my **revision** notes

AQA GCSE

COMPUTER SCIENCE

Steve Cushing

HODDER EDUCATION
AN HACHETTE UK COMPANY

Although every effort has been made to ensure that website addresses are correct at time of going to press, Hodder Education cannot be held responsible for the content of any website mentioned in this book. It is sometimes possible to find a relocated web page by typing in the address of the home page for a website in the URL window of your browser.

Hachette UK's policy is to use papers that are natural, renewable and recyclable products and made from wood grown in sustainable forests. The logging and manufacturing processes are expected to conform to the environmental regulations of the country of origin.

Orders: please contact Bookpoint Ltd, 130 Milton Park, Abingdon, Oxon OX14 4SB.

Telephone: +44 (0)1235 827720. Fax: +44 (0)1235 400454. Lines are open 9.00a.m.–5.00p.m.,

Monday to Saturday, with a 24-hour message answering service. Visit our website at www.hoddereducation.co.uk

First published in 2017 by

Hodder Education,
An Hachette UK Company
Carmelite House
50 Victoria Embankment
London EC4Y 0DZ

Impression number   10   9   8   7   6   5   4   3   2   1

Year   2021   2020   2019   2018   2017

Cover photo © Vladyslav Otsiatsia/Thinkstock/Getty Images

Typeset in India by Aptara, Inc.

Printed in Spain

A catalogue record for this title is available from the British Library

ISBN 978 1 4718 8659 1

Get the most from this book

Everyone has to decide his or her own revision strategy, but it is essential to review your work, learn it and test your understanding. These Revision Notes will help you to do that in a planned way, topic by topic. Use this book as the cornerstone of your revision and don't hesitate to write in it – personalise your notes and check your progress by ticking off each section as you revise.

Tick to track your progress

Use the revision planner on pages 4 and 5 to plan your revision, topic by topic. Tick each box when you have:

● revised and understood a topic
● tested yourself
● practised the exam questions and checked your answers at the back of the book

You can also keep track of your revision by ticking off each topic heading in the book. You may find it helpful to add your own notes as you work through each topic.

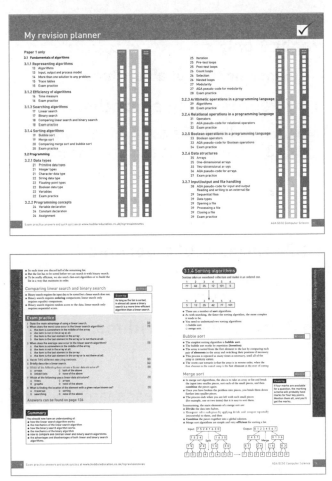

Features to help you succeed

Exam tips

Expert tips are given throughout the book to help you polish your exam technique in order to maximise your chances in the exam.

Exam practice

Practice exam questions are provided for each topic. Use them to consolidate your revision and practise your exam skills.

Summaries

The summaries provide a quick-check bullet list for each topic.

Answers

Answers to exam practice questions can be found at the back of the book.

My revision planner

REVISED   TESTED   EXAM READY

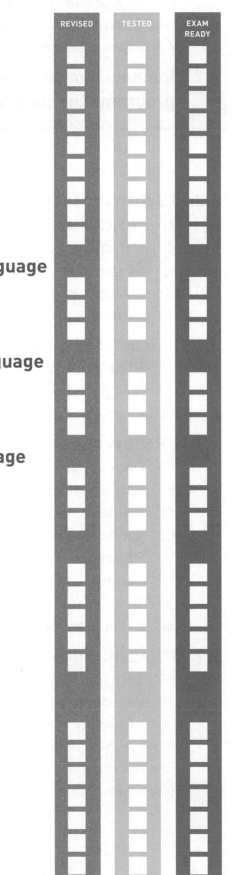

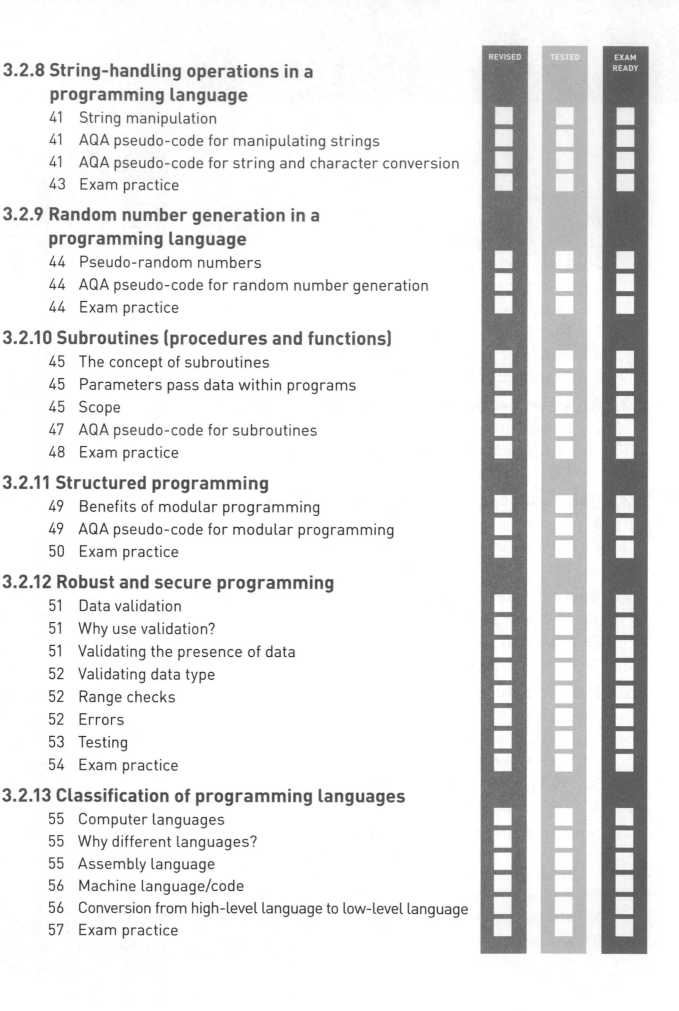

REVISED TESTED EXAM READY

REVISED   TESTED   EXAM READY

Both Papers

3.3 Fundamentals of data representation

3.3.1 Number bases

3.3.2 Converting between number bases

3.3.3 Units of information

3.3.4 Binary arithmetic

3.3.5 Character encoding

3.3.6 Representing images

3.3.7 Representing sound

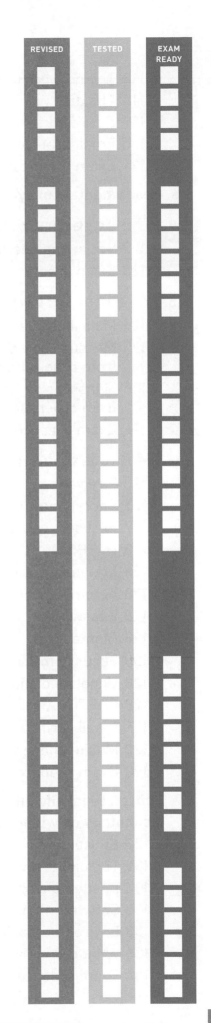

Countdown to my exams

6-8 weeks to go

- Start by looking at the specification — make sure you know exactly what material you need to revise and the style of the examination. Use the revision planner on pages 4–10 to familiarise yourself with the topics.
- Organise your notes, making sure you have covered everything on the specification. The revision planner will help you to group your notes into topics.
- Work out a realistic revision plan that will allow you time for relaxation. Set aside days and times for all the subjects that you need to study, and stick to your timetable.
- Set yourself sensible targets. Break your revision down into focused sessions of around 40 minutes, divided by breaks. These Revision Notes organise the basic facts into short, memorable sections to make revising easier.

REVISED ☐

2-6 weeks to go

- Read through the relevant sections of this book and refer to the exam tips, summaries, and exam practice questions. Tick off the topics as you feel confident about them. Highlight those topics you find difficult and look at them again in detail.
- Make a note of any problem areas as you revise, and ask your teacher to go over these in class.
- Look at past papers. They are one of the best ways to revise and practise your exam skills. Write or prepare planned answers to the exam practice questions provided in this book. Check your answers at the back of the book.
- Use revision activities to try out different revision methods. For example, you can make notes using mind maps, spider diagrams or flash cards.
- Track your progress using the revision planner and give yourself a reward when you have achieved your target.

REVISED ☐

One week to go

- Try to fit in at least one more timed practice of an entire past paper and seek feedback from your teacher, comparing your work closely with the mark scheme.
- Check the revision planner to make sure you haven't missed out any topics. Brush up on any areas of difficulty by talking them over with a friend or getting help from your teacher.
- Attend any revision classes put on by your teacher. Remember, he or she is an expert at preparing people for examinations.

REVISED ☐

The day before the examination

- Flick through these Revision Notes for useful reminders, for example the exam tips, summaries, and exam practice questions.
- Check the time and place of your examination.
- Make sure you have everything you need — extra pens and pencils, tissues, a watch, bottled water, sweets.
- Allow some time to relax and have an early night to ensure you are fresh and alert for the examinations.

REVISED ☐

My exams

Computer Science Paper 1

Date:...

Time:...

Location:...

Computer Science Paper 2

Date:...

Time:...

Location:...

Paper 1 only

3.1 Fundamentals of algorithms

3.1.1 Representing algorithms

Algorithms

- An **algorithm** is a sequence of steps that can be followed to complete a task.
- A computer program is an implementation of an algorithm; an algorithm is not a computer program.
- **Computational thinking** involves learning how to use a set of problem-solving skills and techniques that are used by computer programmers to write algorithms.
- Computational thinking is about considering a problem in a logical way so that a computer could help us to solve it.

Two important techniques used in computational thinking are:

- **Decomposition**: This is breaking a problem into a number of sub-problems, so that each sub-problem accomplishes an identifiable task, which might itself be further subdivided.
- **Abstraction:** This is the process of taking away or removing irrelevant characteristics in terms of the problem being solved in order to reduce it to something simpler to understand.
- In computer science, abstraction is often used for managing the complexity of computer systems. Abstraction is the process of removing **unnecessary detail** from a problem.
- The first step to solving any problem is to decompose the **problem description**.
- A good way to do this would be to **analyse** the problem.
- We can do this in simple steps.

> **Exam tip**
>
> You should always use a systematic approach to problem solving and algorithm creation, representing algorithms using pseudo-code and flowcharts.

> **Exam tip**
>
> The terms in bold used in this guide are important as you will need to demonstrate your understanding of the correct terminology to gain good grades.

Input, output and process model

A computer can be described using a simple model as shown. The **input** stage represents the flow of data into the process from outside the system. The **processing** stage includes all tasks required to effect a transformation of the inputs. The **output** stage is where the data and information flow out of the transformation process.

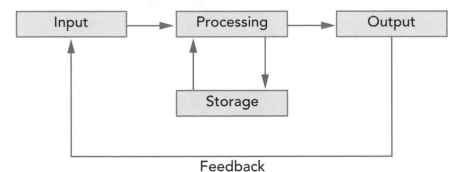

Feedback

Problem: Calculate the volume of a box given its length, width, and height.
- First we identify all the nouns in the problem specification.
- The nouns in the problem describe information that you will need to either identify or keep track of. These nouns can be used to identify:
  ○ input
  ○ output.
- In this problem the nouns are volume, box, length, width and height.
- Length, width and height are our inputs.
- Volume is the output.
- The word 'box' is is irrelevant information for our algorithm. If we now identify all of the verbs in the sentence, in this case 'calculate', we have the process.

So we now have:
- **Inputs**: length, height, width
- **Process**: calculate (in this case this is by multiplying the inputs)
- **Output:** volume

Input and output is shown in AQA pseudo-code as below.

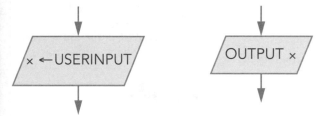

You can now create a step-by-step structured algorithm.

There are several advantages to designing solutions in a **structured** manner.
- One is that it **reduces the complexity**, as each set of steps can act as a separate module (we could call this box Volume and reuse it whenever we want the volume of a box).
- Modularity allows the programmer to tackle problems in a logical fashion. Modules can also be reused.

> **Exam tip**
>
> A structure is a basic unit of programming logic; each structure is a sequence, selection or loop.

More than one solution to any problem

REVISED

- There will always be a number of methods to solve the same problem, but you always need to create **ordered steps** to solve any of these solutions.
- We know there are many answers to the same problem, so what makes the best solution and would lead to the best algorithm?
- The first criteria we need to consider is does the solution:
  ○ work?
  ○ complete the task in a finite (reasonable) amount of time?
- We have lots of solutions to our problem and each, whilst very different, satisfies these two **criteria**.
- Therefore, the next step is to determine which of our solutions is 'best'.
- There are generally two criteria used to determine whether one computer algorithm is 'better' than another and these are:
  ○ the **space** requirements (i.e. how much memory is needed to complete the task)
  ○ the **time** requirements (i.e. how much time it will take to complete the task).

```
USERINPUT length, width, height
volume = length * width * height
OUTPUT volume
```

> **Exam tip**
>
> An algorithm is a sequence of unambiguous instructions for solving a problem (for obtaining a required output for any legitimate input in a finite amount of time). A program is simply an algorithm that has been coded into something that can be run by a computer.

Trace tables

- A **trace table** is a technique used to **test** algorithms to see if any logic errors are occurring whilst the algorithm is being processed.
- Within the table, each column contains a variable and each row displays each numerical input into the algorithm and the resultant values of the variables.

We will look at this in more detail using a Python example:

```
1  y = 2        #variable y = 2
2  x = 2        #variable x = 2
3  y = y + x
```

Trace table:

Line	y	x
1	2	
2	2	2
3	4	2

Exam practice

1 Write the pseudo-code where the user inputs the dimensions of a rectangle and the area of the rectangle is shown on the computer screen. [4]

2 Explain, with simple examples, the basic building blocks of coded solutions. [3]

3 Represent the following code as a simple flowchart. [4]

```
if condition is true
then
    perform instructions in Action1
else
    perform instructions in Action2
endif
```

4 Design a simple flowchart to show the actions of a single move in a child's snakes and ladders game. [6]

5 In which language is a source program usually written? [1]
   A English
   B symbolic
   C high level
   D temporary

Answers can be found on page 135

Summary

You should now have an understanding of:
- the term 'algorithm'
- the term 'decomposition'
- the term 'abstraction'
- simple algorithms in terms of their inputs, processing and outputs

- where inputs, processing and outputs are taking place within an algorithm
- the purpose of simple algorithms
- trace tables and visual inspection to determine how simple algorithms work and what their purpose is.

3.1.2 Efficiency of algorithms

- There are many solutions to the same problem so algorithm **efficiency** is important.
- Some algorithms are more efficient than others. It is obviously better to have an efficient algorithm.
- There are two main measures of the efficiency of an algorithm:
  - time
  - space.
- If it's possible to solve a problem by using a **brute force technique**, you simply try out all the possible combinations of solutions.
- However, if you had to sort words with 158 characters when combined together including spaces, and you could compute 1,000,000,000 possibilities a second, you would still need over 10^149 seconds, which is longer than the expected life of the universe.
- So, to reduce time and make the algorithm more efficient, it is necessary to find a better approach.

Time measure

- **Time measure** is a function describing the amount of time an algorithm takes in terms of the amount of input to the algorithm.
- 'Time' can mean the number of **memory accesses** performed, the number of comparisons between integers, the number of times some inner loop is executed, or some other natural unit related to the amount of real time the algorithm will take.

Exam tip

You will not be expected to carry out formal comparisons of algorithmic efficiency in the exam, and exam questions in this area will only refer to time efficiency.

Exam practice

1 What is meant by the term 'algorithm time efficiency'? [1]
2 What are the TWO criteria that make for a good algorithm? [2]
3 What are the TWO main measures for the efficiency of an algorithm? [1]
    A processor and memory
    B complexity and capacity
    C time and space
    D data and space
4 When determining the efficiency of an algorithm, what is the time factor measured by? [1]
    A counting microseconds
    B counting the number of key operations
    C counting the number of statements
    D counting the kilobytes of the algorithm

Answers can be found on page 135

Summary

You should now have an understanding of:
- how more than one algorithm can be used to solve the same problem
- the efficiency of algorithms; how some algorithms are more efficient than others in solving the same problem.

3.1.3 Searching algorithms

Linear search

- A **linear** search is the most basic search algorithm you can have.
- A linear search moves **sequentially** through your collection (or data structure) looking for a matching value.

> ### Exam tip
>
> There is absolutely no reason to do the questions in the order they are printed in the exam. Do the easiest questions first. Getting one easy question complete at the start of an exam is a wonderful confidence booster.

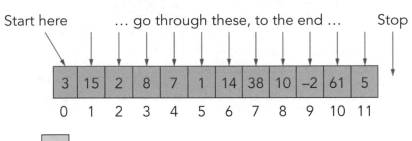

Start here   ... go through these, to the end ...   Stop

| 3 | 15 | 2 | 8 | 7 | 1 | 14 | 38 | 10 | –2 | 61 | 5 |
| 0 | 1 | 2 | 3 | 4 | 5 | 6 | 7 | 8 | 9 | 10 | 11 |

to find 25

- We will not know that there isn't a matching value until the end of the search.

The number we are looking for is called the key. If we have a key of 3, it would look like this, where each line is the next loop in the search.

Key   List

3		6	4	1	9	7	3	2	8
3		6	4	1	9	7	3	2	8
3		6	4	1	9	7	3	2	8
3		6	4	1	9	7	3	2	8
3		6	4	1	9	7	3	2	8
3		6	4	1	9	7	3	2	8

When and if the code finds the key, it stops.

Binary search

- If we need a faster search, we need a completely different algorithm.
- The **binary search** gets its name because the algorithm continually divides the list into two parts.
- It looks at the centre value and disregards anything above or below what we are trying to find.

Let's say we are looking for value 6 from seven ordered items:

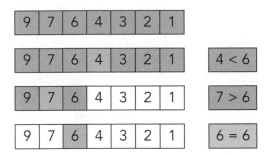

| 9 | 7 | 6 | 4 | 3 | 2 | 1 |

| 9 | 7 | 6 | 4 | 3 | 2 | 1 | 4 < 6

| 9 | 7 | 6 | 4 | 3 | 2 | 1 | 7 > 6

| 9 | 7 | 6 | 4 | 3 | 2 | 1 | 6 = 6

- So each time you discard half of the remaining list.
- But the list has to be sorted before we can search it with binary search.
- To be really efficient, we also need a fast-sort algorithm or to build the list in a way that maintains its order.

Comparing linear search and binary search

REVISED

- Binary search requires the input data to be sorted but a linear search does not.
- Binary search requires **ordering** comparisons; linear search only requires equality comparisons.
- Binary search requires random access to the data; linear search only requires sequential access.

Exam tip

As long as the list is sorted, in almost all cases a binary search is a more time-efficient algorithm than a linear search.

Exam practice

1 State the main advantage of using a linear search. [2]
2 When does the worst case occur in the linear search algorithm? [1]
   A   the item is somewhere in the middle of the array
   B   the item is not in the array at all
   C   the item is the last element in the array
   D   the item is the last element in the array or is not there at all
3 When does the average case occur in the linear search algorithm? [1]
   A   the item is somewhere in the middle of the array
   B   the item is not in the array at all
   C   the item is the last element in the array
   D   the item is the last element in the array or is not there at all
4 Name TWO different searching methods. [2]
5 Briefly describe a linear search. [4]
6 Which of the following does not use a linear data structure? [1]
   A   arrays   C   both of the above
   B   linked lists   D   none of the above
7 Which of the following uses a linear data structure? [1]
   A   trees   C   arrays
   B   graphs   D   none of the above
8 What is finding the location of the element with a given value known as? [1]
   A   traversal   C   sorting
   B   searching   D   none of the above

Answers can be found on page 135

Summary

You should now have an understanding of:
- how the linear search algorithm works
- the mechanics of the linear search algorithm
- how the binary search algorithm works
- the mechanics of the binary algorithm
- how to compare and contrast linear and binary search algorithms
- the advantages and disadvantages of both linear and binary search algorithms.

3.1.4 Sorting algorithms

Sorting takes an unordered collection and makes it an ordered one.

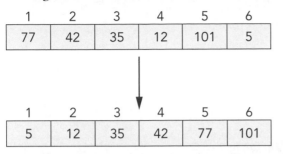

1	2	3	4	5	6
77	42	35	12	101	5

1	2	3	4	5	6
5	12	35	42	77	101

- There are a number of **sort** algorithms.
- As with searching, the faster the sorting algorithm, the more complex it tends to be.
- You need to understand two sorting algorithms:
  - ○ bubble sort
  - ○ merge sort.

Bubble sort

REVISED

- The simplest sorting algorithm is **bubble sort**.
- The bubble sort works by repetition (**iteration**).
- The array is sorted from the first element to the last by comparing each pair of **elements** in the array and switching their positions if necessary.
- This process is repeated as many times as necessary, until all of the array is correctly sorted.
- The worst-case scenario is that the array is in reverse order, when the first element in the sorted array is the **last element** at the start of sorting.

Merge sort

REVISED

- In merge sort algorithms, the idea is to take an array or list and break the input into smaller pieces, sort each of the small pieces, and then **combine** the pieces again.
- Once you have broken the problem into pieces, you break them down further into smaller pieces.
- The process ends when you are left with such small pieces (for example, one or two items) that it is easy to sort them.

Exam tip

If four marks are available for a question, the marking scheme will probably have marks for four key points. Mention them all, and you'll get the marks.

Summarising, the main elements of a merge sort are:
- **Divide** the data into halves.
- **Conquer**: solve each piece by applying divide-and-conquer repeatedly (recursively) to them, and then
- **Combine** the pieces together into a global solution.
- Merge sort algorithms are simple and very **efficient** for sorting a list.

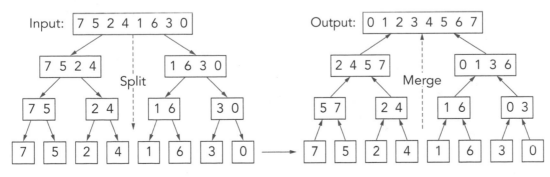

Comparing merge sort and bubble sort

- In almost all cases, merge sort will **take a lot less time** than bubble sort to sort the data.
- Bubble sort is not efficient in terms of time but is quite good in terms of memory as the data is sorted within the list, whereas merge sort is much more time efficient but generally uses more memory as copies of the lists are created as they are split up.

Exam practice

1 What is the operation of processing each element in a list known as? [1]
   A   sorting
   B   merging
   C   inserting
   D   traversal
2 Briefly describe a bubble sort. [4]
3 What is merge sort? [2]
4 The arranging of data in a logical sequence is called ... [1]
   A   sorting
   B   classifying
   C   reproducing
   D   summarising

Answers can be found on page 135

Summary

You should now have an understanding of:
- how the merge sort algorithm works
- the mechanics of the merge sort algorithm
- how the bubble sort algorithm works
- the mechanics of the bubble sort algorithm
- how to compare and contrast merge sort and bubble sort algorithms
- the advantages and disadvantages of both merge and bubble sort algorithms.

3.2 Programming

3.2.1 Data types

- Computers are machines that **process** data.
- Data is stored in the computer's memory in **variables**.
- Variables have a **name**, **data type** and **value**.

Exam tip

If you get stuck on a question, move on. Start doing another one.

Primitive data types

REVISED

- The most common types of data, and the ones you will be using, are called **primitive** data types.
- Primitive data types are **predefined** types of data, which are supported by the programming language.
- Data can be stored in many different forms and the proper term for these forms is data types.

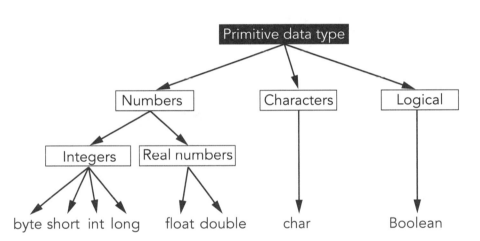

- The data type determines what actions, for instance, searching, sorting or calculating, can be performed on the data when it is held within a field of a database or a spreadsheet.

Integer types

REVISED

Integer data types deal with **whole numbers** not decimal numbers.

An integer is a whole number (not a fractional number). It can be **positive**, **negative**, or **zero**.

Integer data types:
- represent whole numbers
- may be signed or unsigned
- have a range of values, depending on the size of memory used.

Character data type

REVISED

Another primitive data type is **char**. This is simply a character, for example, 'a'.

Character data types:
- represent **symbolic** information
- are declared by the **char** key word
- give each symbol a corresponding integer code
- take 16 bits of memory if you are using a single two-byte (16-bit) Unicode character.

String data type

REVISED

A string variable is a sequence of **alphanumeric characters** and allowed symbols that are contained within quotation marks. "Hello world" is an example of a string. Strings can also be contained within single quotes. Strings are basically boxes used for storing text.

String data types:
- represent a **sequence** of characters
- are declared by the **string** key word
- have a default value **null** (no value)
- are enclosed in quotes
- can be **concatenated** using the + operator.

Floating-point types

REVISED

A floating-point number *does* have a **decimal point**.

Floating-point data types:
- represent **real** numbers
- may be **signed** or **unsigned**
- have a range of values and different precision depending on the memory used
- can behave abnormally in calculations.

> **Exam tip**
>
> Real numbers may also be described as floating-point.

Boolean data type

REVISED

Boolean data types:
- are declared by the **bool** key word
- have two possible values: **true** and **false**
- are useful in logical expressions
- have the default value false.

Variables

REVISED

A variable is:
- a **placeholder** of information that can usually be changed at run-time.

Variables allow you to:
- store information
- retrieve the stored information
- **manipulate** the stored information.

Exam practice

1 What will the following pseudo-code do? [1]

```
INT_TO_STRING(16)
```

2 What will the following pseudo-code do? [1]

```
REAL_TO_STRING(16.3)
```

3 In mathematics which of the following are integers? [7]

8, 5 103, −1.33, 1 3/4, 98, 3.14, 1 500.45, −9, 3, 5

4 Give TWO reasons why the integer data type would be used in programming rather than
using the real data type. [2]

5 What is a real data type? [2]

6 What will the following pseudo-code do? [1]

```
STRING_TO_REAL('16.3')
```

7 Give TWO reasons why a programmer would wish to use integer data types rather than real
data types. [2]

8 What will the following pseudo-code do? [1]

```
STRING_TO_ INT('16')
```

Answers can be found on page 136

Summary

You should now have an understanding of:
● the concept of a data type
● how to use the following data types appropriately:
  – integer
  – real
  – Boolean
  – character
  – string.

3.2.2 Programming concepts

The three combining principles (**sequence**, **iteration/repetition** and **selection/choice**) are basic to all imperative programming languages.

Exam tip

Identifier names include names for variables, constants and subroutines.

Variable declaration

REVISED

You can also **assign** a variable a value on the same line as you **declare** it:

```
int a
a = 2
```

is the same as:

```
int a = 2
```

This is called **initialisation**.

Variables only hold one value at a time:

```
number = 1
print number
number = 2
print number
```

This will print:

```
1
2
```

After these statements, the variable **number** will hold only the value of 2; the value 1 is not kept.

Constant declaration

REVISED

A constant declaration specifies the **name**, **data type** and **value** of the constant.

Unlike a variable, a constant holds a value that *does not change*.

Assignment

REVISED

Assignment is the process of setting the value of a variable.

A variable can be assigned different values during a program's execution, hence the name, 'variable'.

Syntax:

```
Variable ← <add value here>
```

Example

```
Counter ← 0
```

and:

```
myString ← 'Hello world'
```

Iteration

Iterations are also called **loops**.

Loops/iteration statements are used to repeat the execution of statement or blocks.

There are two types of loop/iteration structures and these are:
- **pre-test loops** and **post-test loops**
- loops that depend on reaching a maximum number of **iterations** or 'counts' (counter-controlled loops).

> **Exam tip**
>
> A theoretical understanding of condition(s) at either end of an iterative structure is required in the exam, regardless of whether they are supported by the language(s) being used.

Pre-test loops

When encountering a pre-test loop, the computer tests the **condition** *before* the loop body executes. For example, FOR and WHILE loops. Programmers use pre-test loops when the loop might never need to execute at all.

The loop has three parts.
- The initialiser is executed at the start of the loop.
- The loop condition is tested before iteration to decide whether to continue or terminate the loop.
- The increment is executed after the test.

> **Example**
>
> A pre-test WHILE loop
> ```
> x ← 0
> WHILE x < 3
>     x ← x + 1
>     OUTPUT "Hello"
> ENDWHILE
> ```
> Output:
> ```
> Hello
> Hello
> Hello
> ```

Post-test loops

A post-test condition is tested *after* each iteration to check if the loop should continue (at least a single iteration occurs).

When encountering a post-test loop, the computer tests the condition after the loop body executes.

Programmers use post-test loops when they want the loop body to execute at least once.
```
REPEAT
    OUTPUT "Who will win this years World Cup?"
    USERINPUT ← userAnswer
UNTIL userAnswer = "England"
OUTPUT "You have wisdom."
```

Count loops

REVISED

A count-controlled loop iterates a **specific number of times**.

```
FOR Count ← 1 Step 1 To 5
    Write Count
ENDFOR
```

Selection

REVISED

Selection is about making a **decision**. We have just shown a decision in the count loop. Decisions are usually **Boolean** so they can be true or false. Let's say we want a condition where if a student's grade is greater than or equal to 60 we want the system to print 'Passed'.

```
IF grade ≥ 60:
    OUTPUT "Passed"
ENDIF
```

We can expand on this code by adding an ELSE statement:

```
IF grade ≥ 60
THEN
    OUTPUT "Passed"
ELSE
    OUTPUT "Failed"
ENDIF
```

Nested loops

REVISED

Nested loops consist of an **outer loop** and **one or more inner loops**. Each time the outer loop is repeated, the inner loops are re-entered and started again as if new.

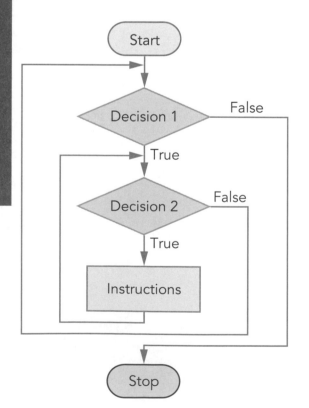

```
WHILE NotSolved
    <instructions here>
    FOR i ← 1 TO 10      # this is the nested iteration
          <instructions here>
    ENDFOR
    <instructions here>
ENDWHILE
```

Modularity

There are several advantages to designing solutions in a **structured** manner.

One is that it reduces the complexity, as each set of steps can act as a separate module.

Modularity allows the programmer to tackle problems in a **logical** fashion.

Modules can also be reused. Modules are a type of subroutine.

A subroutine is simply a **sequence of instructions** that is set up to perform a frequently required task.
● Code in a subroutine is **reusable**.
● A subroutine can provide a general solution for different situations.
● A well-defined task can be done in a subroutine, making the main script simpler and easier to read and understand.

AQA pseudo-code for modularity

If

```
IF BoolExp THEN
    <statements here>
ENDIF
```

Example

```
a ← 1
IF (a MOD 2) = 0 THEN
    OUTPUT 'even'
ENDIF
```

> **Exam tip**
>
> Make sure that you fully understand the AQA pseudo-code used in this book; it will be used in the coded examination questions.

If-else

```
IF BoolExp THEN
    <statements here>
ELSE
    <statements here>
ENDIF
```

Example

```
a ← 1
IF (a MOD 2) = 0 THEN
    OUTPUT 'even'
ELSE
    OUTPUT 'odd'
ENDIF
```

Else-if

```
IF BoolExp THEN
    <statements here>
ELSE IF BoolExp THEN
    <statements here>
    <possibly more ELSE IFs>
ELSE
    <statements here>
ENDIF
```

Example

```
a ← 1
IF (a MOD 4) = 0 THEN
    OUTPUT 'multiple of 4'
ELSE IF (a MOD 4) = 1 THEN
    OUTPUT 'leaves a remainder of 1'
ELSE IF (a MOD 4) = 2 THEN
    OUTPUT 'leaves a remainder of 2'
ELSE
    OUTPUT 'leaves a remainder of 3'
ENDIF
```

Exam practice

1 Write the pseudo-code to output the numbers 1 to 50 inclusive using a WHILE loop. [4]

2 Write the pseudo-code to output the numbers 1 to 60 inclusive using a FOR loop. [2]

3 Briefly describe the term 'module'. [2]

4 Write the pseudo-code to ask the user to input two values into variables for start and finish, then print the integers from start to finish inclusive using a FOR loop. [6]

5 Write the pseudo-code to ask the user to input two values into variables for start and finish, then print the integers from start to finish inclusive using a FOR loop, but if start is bigger than finish output an error message instead! [8]

6 Write the pseudo-code to create a REPEAT-UNTIL iteration to output 1 to 6. [5]

7 Write the pseudo-code to create a WHILE iteration to output 1 to 3. [5]

8 Write the pseudo-code to create a FOR iteration to output 1 to 3. [5]

Answers can be found on page 136

Summary

You should now have an understanding of:
- how the following statement types can be combined in programs:
  - variable declaration
  - constant declaration
  - assignment
  - iteration
  - selection
  - subroutine (procedure/function)
- how to write programs using these statement types

- how to interpret algorithms that include these statement types
- why named constants and variables are used
- how to use definite and indefinite iteration, including indefinite iteration with the condition(s) at the start or the end of the iterative structure
- how to use meaningful identifier names and why it is important to use them.

Algorithms

- The study of **algorithms** did not start with the invention of computers, e.g. adding two numbers together is a mathematical problem.
- When the term 'algorithm' is used in mathematics, it refers to a set of steps used to solve a mathematical problem.

The algorithms for performing long division or multiplication are good examples. If you were carrying out a long division for 52 divided by 3 you would have the following specific sequence of steps and their outcomes:

- How many times does 3 go into 52?
  - The answer is 17 ($3 \times 17 = 51$).
- How many are left over?
  - The answer is 1.
- How many times does 3 go into 10?
  - The answer is 3 with 1 left over.

And, of course, the answer becomes 17.3333333

The **step-by-step process** used to do the long division is called a long division algorithm. Algorithms are used a lot in mathematics, especially in **algebra**.

Differences

There are some important differences that you must understand.

Mathematics	Computer science
The following instructions are the same in mathematics. A = B B = A In mathematics both these instructions would express that A and B are equal, so they have the same purpose.	In computer science = is used for assignment, so A = B copies the value of B into A, whereas B = A copies the value of A into B.
In mathematics we work with relations. A relation B = A + 1 means that it is true all the time.	In computer science we work with assignments. We can have: A = 5 B = A + 1 A = 3 The relation B = A + 1 is true only after the second instruction and before the third one. After the third one A = 3, but B is still 6.
The instruction A = A + 3 is false in mathematics. It cannot exist.	In computer science A = A + 3 means: the new value of A is equal to the old one plus three.
The instruction A + 6 = 3 is allowed in mathematics (it is an equation).	A + 6 = 3 has no meaning in computer science where the = is used for assignment as then the left side must be a variable so we would have to say three = A + 6. In some languages we could use the following to see if they are equal A + 6 == 3

Integer division, including remainders is usually a two-stage process and uses modular arithmetic, e.g. the calculation 11/2 would generate the following values:

Integer division: the integer quotient of 11 divided by 2 (11 DIV 2) = 5

Remainder: the remainder when 11 is divided by 2 (11 MOD 2) = 1

AQA pseudo-code for arithmetic operations

REVISED ☐

- standard arithmetic operations: +, −
- the * symbol is used instead of × for multiplication
- the / symbol is used instead of ÷ for division (for integer division use DIV)
- standard use of brackets to make precedence obvious.

Exam practice

1 The basic operations performed by a computer are ...   [1]
   A   arithmetic operation
   B   logical operation
   C   storage and relative
   D   all the above

2 Fill in the missing descriptions in the table below.   [4]

Operator	Description
+	
−	
*	
/	

3 Write the pseudo-code to create an integer division of 9 divided by 5.   [1]

4 Write the pseudo-code to create the remainder of 9 divided by 5.   [1]

Answers can be found on page 136

Summary

You should now have an understanding of:
- these arithmetic operations:
  - addition
  - subtraction
  - multiplication
  - real division
  - integer division, including remainders.

Operators

In order to program you will need to understand the **syntax** for mathematic operators.

Specifically the operators for:
- **calculation**
- selection.

Calculation

Operator	Meaning	Type	Example
+	Addition	Binary	a = b + c;
–	Subtraction	Binary	a = b – c;
*	Multiplication	Binary	a = b * c;
/	Division	Binary	a = b / c;
%	Modulus	Binary	a = b % c;
–	Negation	Unary	a = –b;

Selection

Operator	Meaning
>	Greater than
<	Less than
=	Equal to
≥	Greater than or equal to
≤	Less than or equal to
≠	Not equal to

AQA pseudo-code for relational operators

Less than

```
Exp < Exp
4 < 6
```

Greater than

```
Exp > Exp
4.1 > 4.0
```

Equal to

```
Exp = Exp
3 = 3
```

Not equal to

```
Exp ≠ Exp
True ≠ False
```

Less than or equal to

```
Exp ≤ Exp
3 ≤ 4
4 ≤ 4
```

Greater than or equal to

```
Exp ≥ Exp
4 ≥ 3
4.5 ≥ 4.5
```

Exam tip

Remember to read each question carefully. The stress of the examination can cause you to misread a question.

Exam tip

Remember, the exams are not designed to trick you. Convince yourself that you know how to answer exam questions and you're almost there.

Exam practice

1 Write the pseudo-code where the user inputs the dimensions of a rectangle and the area and perimeter of the rectangle is shown on the computer screen. [6]

2 Write the pseudo-code to ask the user to input a number and output to the screen whether it is an odd or even number. [6]

3 Complete the chart shown by adding the descriptions. One has been done for you. [5]

Operator	Description
>	Greater than
<	
=	
≥	
≤	
≠	

4 Write the pseudo-code where the user inputs the length of the side of a square and its area is shown on the screen. Produce an error message if the length entered by the user is negative. [5]

5 Write the pseudo-code where the user inputs three numbers and either 'all 3 equal' or 'not all equal' is shown on the screen. [6]

6 Write the pseudo-code where the user inputs three numbers and the largest number entered is shown on the screen. [8]

Answers can be found on page 136

Summary

You should now have an understanding of:
- these relational operators:
  - equal to
  - not equal to
  - less than
  - greater than
  - less than or equal to
  - greater than or equal to.

You must be able to use these operators within their own programs and be able to interpret them when used within algorithms. Note that different languages may use different symbols to represent these operators.

3.2.5 Boolean operations in a programming language

Boolean operators

AND

The **AND** operator ensures that **all the conditions are true** before returning a value.

OR

The **OR** operator requires **at least one of the specified conditions to be true**. In searches, you use OR to retrieve records or pages that contains **either** of two or more terms. The OR operator is generally used to assess similar, equivalent or synonymous conditions.

NOT

The **NOT** operator **inverts** the value of a Boolean expression. Thus if b is true, x is false. If b is false, x is true.

AQA pseudo-code for Boolean operations

Logical AND

```
BoolExp AND BoolExp
```

Example

```
(3 = 3) AND (3 ≤ 4)
```

Logical OR

```
BoolExp OR BoolExp
```

Example

```
(x < 1) OR (x > 9)
```

> **Exam tip**
>
> AQA use the following symbols: =, ≠, <, >, ≤, ≥

Logical NOT

```
NOT BoolExp
```

Example

```
NOT (another _ go = False)
```

Condition-controlled iteration

Repeat-until

(Repeat the statements until the Boolean expression is True.)

```
REPEAT
   < statements here >
UNTIL BoolExp
```

Example

```
a ← 1
REPEAT
   OUTPUT a
   a ← a + 1
UNTIL a = 4                    # will output 1, 2, 3
```

While

(While the Boolean expression is True, repeat the statements.)

```
WHILE BoolExp
   < statements here >
ENDWHILE
```

Example

```
a ← 1
WHILE a < 4
   OUTPUT a
   a ← a + 1
ENDWHILE                        # will output 1, 2, 3
```

Exam practice

1 Write the following sentence as a Boolean expression. [2]

   When the door is open and it is cold outside I have to wear
   my coat.

2 Write pseudo-code using a repeat loop and a Boolean expression
   to print out all the even numbers from 2 to 100. [5]

3 What is a Boolean data type? [4]

Answers can be found on page 137

Summary

You should now have an understanding of:
● these Boolean operators:
   - NOT
   - AND
   - OR.

You must be able to use these operators, and combinations of these
operators, within conditions for iterative and selection structures.

3.2.6 Data structures

Arrays

In programming, one of the most important design decisions involves which **data structure** to use.

- **Arrays** and **linked lists** are among the most common data structures, and each is applicable in different situations.
- Arrays and linked lists are both designed to store multiple elements, most often of the **same type**.
- An array is an ordered **arrangement** of data elements that are accessed by referencing their location within the array and a linked list is a group of elements, each of which contains a **pointer** that **concurrently** points to the following element.

One-dimensional arrays

- An array is a series of elements of the same type placed in **contiguous memory** locations that can be individually referenced by adding an **index** to a **unique identifier**.

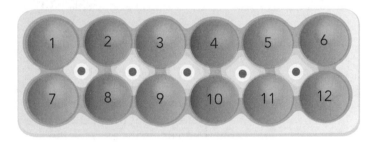

> **Exam tip**
>
> Manage your time. The number of marks are important – normally one mark relates to about one minute. This is where you need to be strict on yourself, you MUST move on once you have spent enough time on a question or you won't be able to give the next question your full attention.

- An array is a data structure made up of a series of variables all of the same type, grouped under one identifier. Elements are accessed using an **index**.
- A one-dimensional array is a data structure that allows a list of items to be stored with the capability of accessing each item by pointing to its location within the array.

Two-dimensional arrays

- Two-dimensional arrays are a little more complex than one-dimensional arrays, but really they are nothing more than an **array of arrays**, in other words an array in one row and another in the next row.

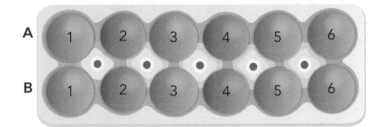

- The best way of understanding a two-dimensional array is to think of it as a way of holding and accessing information within a matrix or grid made up of rows and columns, such as the one shown.

	0	1	2	3
0	A	B	C	D
1	E	F	G	H
2	I	J	K	L
3	M	N	O	P
4	Q	R	S	T

AQA pseudo-code for arrays

REVISED

Assignment

```
Identifier ← [Exp, Exp, …, Exp]
```

Example

```
primes ← [2, 3, 5, 7, 11, 13]
```

Accessing an element

```
Identifier[IntExp]
```

Example

```
primes[0]
# evaluates to 2 (questions on exam
# papers will always state whether
# indexing begins at 0 or 1, here 0
# has been assumed)
```

Updating an element

```
Identifier[IntExp] ← Exp
```

Example

```
primes[5] ← 17          # array is now  [2,3,5,7,11,17]
```

Exam tip

Whilst you do not have to use the AQA pseudo-code in your answers you must ensure that the pseudo-code you do use is easy for the examiner to understand.

Accessing an element in a two-dimensional array

```
Identifier[IntExp][IntExp]
```

Example
```
tables ← [ [1, 2, 3],
           [2, 4, 6],
           [3, 6, 9],
           [4, 8, 12] ]
tables[3][1]
# evaluates to 8 as second element
# (with index 1) of fourth array
# (with index 3) in tables is 8
```

Updating an element in a two-dimensional array

```
Identifier[IntExp][IntExp] ← Exp
```

Example
```
tables[3][1] ← 16
# tables is now
#[  [1, 2, 3],
#   [2, 4, 6],
#   [3, 6, 9],
#   [4, 16, 12] ]
```

Array length

```
LEN(Identifier)
```

Example
```
LEN(primes)    # evaluates to 6 using example above
LEN(tables)    # evaluates to 4 using example above
LEN(tables[0]) # evaluates to 3 using example above
```

Exam practice

1 Write the pseudo-code to create a one-dimensional array containing the following numbers: 2, 3, 5, 7, 11, 13. [1]

2 Arrays are the best data structures for ... [1]
  A relatively permanent collections of data
  B when the size of the structure and the data in the structure are constantly changing
  C both of the above situations
  D none of the above situations

3 Write the pseudo-code to change the number 13 to 17 in the array in Question 1. [1]

4 What is meant by initialising an array? [1]

5 Explain, using an example, the term 'one-dimensional array'. [1]

6 Explain the difference between single and two-dimensional arrays. [2]

7 Why is the first element in an array often 0 not 1? [1]

8 Explain why the elements of an array are stored successively in memory. [1]

9 Write the pseudo-code to create a two-dimensional array with the following numbers: [1]

1, 2, 3

2, 4, 6

3, 6, 9

4, 8, 12

10 Given the array shown below and an index of 1, what number will tables[3][1] equate to? [1]

```
tables ← [[1,  2,  3],
          [2,  4,  6],
          [9,  6,  9],
          [4,  8, 12]]
```

Answers can be found on page 137

Summary

You should now have an understanding of:
- the concept of data structures
- how to use arrays (or equivalent) in the design of solutions to simple problems
- how to use records (or equivalent) in the design of solutions to simple problems.

3.2.7 Input/output and file handling

Let's look at how we show an input from a keyboard and output to a screen in our code:

Flowchart	Pseudo-code	Python 3
x ←USERINPUT	x ← USERINPUT	x = input()

Flowchart	Pseudo-code	Python 3
OUTPUT x	OUTPUT x	print(x)

AQA pseudo-code for input and output

REVISED

Input

```
USERINPUT
```

Example
```
a ← USERINPUT
```

Output

```
OUTPUT StringExp
```

Example
```
OUTPUT a
```

Reading and writing to an external file

REVISED

A file is a permanent way to store data.

Three types of file can be used for storing data:
- sequential
- random
- binary.

Sequential files are useful for:
- storing text
- easy implementation in programs
- where real-time editing of the file(s) is not required.

Random file structures are useful for:
- files that require real-time editing
- storing records.

Binary files are useful for:
- storing numbers, programs and images
- where no defined file structure is present.

Sequential files

REVISED

Sequential files are stored like a one-dimensional array but they are read from start to finish and so cannot be read and written to simultaneously.

They are readable across systems because:
- they have a universal standard format that is used in all text editors
- numerical data is always stored as a string, for example, 5.32 would be stored as '5.32'.

Data types

REVISED

Data is *always* written and retrieved as **characters**.

Hence, any number written in this mode will result in the ASCII value of the number being stored.

For example, the number 17 is stored as two separate characters, '1' and '7'. Which means that 17 is stored as [49 55] and not as [17].

Files are manipulated in three stages:
- open file
- process file
- close file.

Opening a file

REVISED

If the file does not exist it is created and then opened by the operating system. A portion of memory (RAM) is reserved for the file by the operating system.

Processing a file

REVISED

When a file is open it can be written to or read from (both in the case of random and binary files).

Writing to a file will save it to backing store.

Closing a file

REVISED

When a file has been opened and processed it must then be closed. The operating system will then release the memory.

Exam practice

1 Briefly describe an exported sequential text file. [6]
2 Briefly explain the difference between a sequential file and a random access file. [6]

Answers can be found on page 138

Summary

You should now have an understanding of:
- how to obtain user input from the keyboard
- how to output data and information from a program to the computer display
- how to read/write from/to a text file.

3.2.8 String-handling operations in a programming language

String manipulation

REVISED

- A string is simply a list of characters in order, where a character can be anything a user can type on the keyboard in a **single keystroke**.
- An empty string is a string that has zero characters.
- Most code recognises as strings everything that is delimited by quotation marks (either " " or ' ').
- We can also manipulate strings using some built-in methods.

AQA pseudo-code for manipulating strings

REVISED

String length

```
LEN(StringExp)
```

Example

```
LEN('computer science')  # evaluates to 16 (including
                         ~ space)
```

Position of a character

```
POSITION(StringExp, CharExp)
```

Example

```
POSITION('computer science', 'm')
# evaluates to 2 (as with arrays,
# exam papers will make it clear
# whether indexing starts at 0 or
# 1, here 0 has been assumed)
```

Substring

```
SUBSTRING(IntExp, IntExp, StringExp)
```

The substring is created by the first parameter indicating the start position within the string, the second parameter indicating the final position within the string and the third parameter being the string itself.

Example

```
SUBSTRING(2, 9, 'computer science')
# evaluates to 'mputer s'
```

Concatenation

```
StringExp + StringExp
```

Example

```
'computer' + 'science'  # evaluates to 'computerscience'
```

3.2.8 String-handling operations in a programming language

AQA pseudo-code for string and character conversion

Converting string to integer

```
STRING_TO_INT(StringExp)
```

Example

```
STRING_TO_INT('16')   # evaluates to the integer 16
```

Converting string to real

```
STRING_TO_REAL(StringExp)
```

Example

```
STRING_TO_REAL('16.3')   # evaluates to the real 16.3
```

Converting integer to string

```
INT_TO_STRING(IntExp)
```

Example

```
INT_TO_STRING(16)     # evaluates to the string '16'
```

Converting real to string

```
REAL_TO_STRING(RealExp)
```

Example

```
REAL_TO_STRING(16.3)      # evaluates to the string
                          # '16.3'
```

Converting character to character code

```
CHAR_TO_CODE(CharExp)
```

Example

```
CHAR_TO_CODE('a')  # evaluates to 97 using  ASCII/Unicode
```

Converting character code to character

```
CODE_TO_CHAR(IntExp)
```

Example

```
CODE_TO_CHAR(97)  # evaluates to 'a' using  ASCII/Unicode
```

Exam practice

1 In programming what is a string? [4]

2 What will the following pseudo-code evaluate to? [1]

```
SUBSTRING(4, 10, 'computer science')
```

3 What will the following pseudo-code evaluate to? [1]

```
'programming' + 'is' + 'cool'
```

4 What will the following pseudo-code do? [1]

```
STRING_TO_REAL(1.3)
```

Answers can be found on page 138

Summary

You should now have an understanding of:
- these string-handling operations:
    - length
    - position
    - substring
    - concatenation
    - convert character to character code
    - convert character code to character
- these string-conversion operations:
    - string to integer
    - string to real
    - integer to string
    - real to string.

3.2.9 Random number generation in a programming language

Pseudo-random numbers

- You can program a machine to generate what can be called '**random**' numbers,
- Because the machine is following the same algorithm to generate them, these numbers will follow a pattern.
- The results are normally sufficiently complex to make the pattern difficult to identify.
- Because it is ruled by a carefully defined and consistently repeated algorithm, the numbers it produces are not truly random. They are what we call '**pseudo-random**' numbers.

> **Exam tip**
>
> Start answering the questions that you feel most confident about. There is no need to answer the questions in order.

AQA pseudo-code for random number generation

Random integer generation (between two integers inclusively)

```
RANDOM_INT(IntExp, IntExp)
```

Example

```
RANDOM_INT(3, 5)    # will randomly generate 3, 4 or 5
```

Exam practice

1 What will the following pseudo-code do? [1]

```
RANDOM_INT(2, 8)
```

2 Why are random numbers generated in a program sometimes referred to as pseudo-random numbers? [6]

3 Why do programmers need to generate random numbers? [6]

Answers can be found on page 138

Summary

You should now have an understanding of:
- random number generation
- how to use random number generation within your computer programs.

3.2.10 Subroutines (procedures and functions)

The concept of subroutines

- You need to break sections of code into separate **logical** units.
- The code associated with **accomplishing** each task should be separated from the code that accomplishes other tasks.
- These actions are referred to as events and are one way of breaking up code into smaller, more logical units.
- Another way to break up an application is by using either **functions** or **subroutines**.

Advantages of using subroutines in programs

- Programs are made more readable by breaking large amounts of code into smaller, more concise parts.
- By breaking code into functions and subroutines, code can be written once and **reused** often.
- This reduces the size of the application and reduces **debugging** time.
- Functions and subroutines operate similarly but they have one key difference:
  - a function is used when a **value is returned** to the calling routine
  - a subroutine is used when a desired task is needed, but **no value is returned**.

> **Exam tip**
>
> Structure your answer. Don't just jump into writing your answer.

Parameters pass data within programs

Parameters:
- are the names of the information that we want to use in a function or procedure
- allow us to pass information or instructions into functions and procedures
- are useful when we are using number information.

Parameter values passed into functions are called **arguments.**
- Subroutines return values to the **calling routine**.
- Parameter passing is the mechanism used to pass parameters to a procedure (subroutine) or function.
- The most common method is to pass the value of the actual parameter which is referred to as '**to call by value**'.
- It is also possible to pass the address of the **memory** location where the actual parameter is stored and this is referred to as '**to call by reference**'.

Scope

You will need to understand scope in order to use subroutines effectively as local variables usually:
- **only exist while the subroutine is executing**
- are only accessible within the subroutine.

Variable scope

- A variable's scope consists of all code blocks in which it is visible.
- A variable is considered visible if it can be accessed by statements within that code block.

Local scope

- Local scope is limited to the block where the variable is declared.
- A block is the body of a control structure, the body of a function, or a place such as the file or string with the code where the variable is declared.

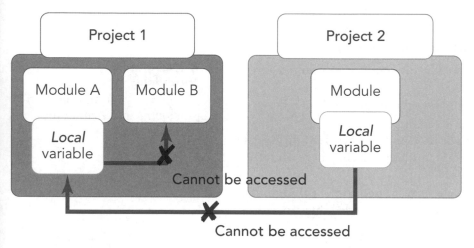

- Different subroutines can have local variables with the same names because the functions cannot access each other's local variables.

Global scope

- Global variables can be accessed from anywhere.

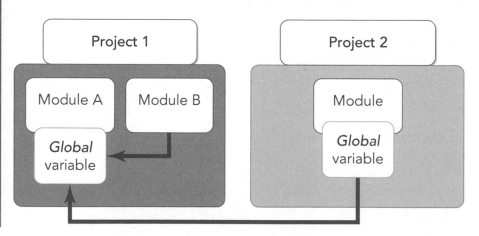

- In most programming languages variables are treated as global if not declared as local.
- In Python it is the opposite. Variables are local if not declared as global.

Why is it better to use local scope?

It is good programming style to use local variables whenever possible. This helps to avoid **cluttering** the global environment with unnecessary names. Other benefits of using local scope include:

- The **source code** is easier to understand when the scope of individual elements is limited.
- Subroutines can be more easily reused if their variables are all local.
- Global variables can be read or modified by any part of the program. A global variable can be **accessed** or set by any part of the program, and any rules regarding its use can easily be broken or forgotten.
- Global names are also available everywhere. You may unknowingly end up using a global variable when you think you are using a local variable.
- Testing your code is harder if you use global variables.

AQA pseudo-code for subroutines

REVISED

Subroutine definition

```
SUBROUTINE Identifier(parameters)
    <statements here>
ENDSUBROUTINE
```

Example

```
SUBROUTINE show_add(a, b)
    result ← a + b
    OUTPUT result
ENDSUBROUTINE
SUBROUTINE say_hi()
    OUTPUT 'hi'
ENDSUBROUTINE
```

Subroutine return value

```
RETURN Exp
```

Example

```
SUBROUTINE add(a, b)
    result ← a + b
    RETURN result
ENDSUBROUTINE
```

> **Exam tip**
>
> Don't forget to attempt all questions. This is the best way to gain high marks in an exam.

Calling a subroutine

```
Identifier(parameters)
```

Example

```
show_add(2, 3)
answer ← add(2, 3)
```

Exam practice

1 What is a function?   [2]

2 What does the term "word length" refer to?   [2]

3 What is meant by a calling function?   [2]

4 What is an argument?   [1]

5 What are actual parameters?   [2]

6 What are formal parameters?   [2]

7 How is a function invoked?   [2]

8 What are local variables?   [2]

9 What are global variables?   [4]

Answers can be found on page 138

Summary

You should now have an understanding of:
- a subroutine being a named 'out of line' block of code that may be executed (called) by simply writing its name in a program statement
- the advantages of using subroutines in programs
- the use of parameters to pass data within programs
- how to use subroutines that require more than one parameter
- how data is passed to a subroutine using parameters
- how to use subroutines that return values to the calling routine
- how data is passed out of a subroutine using return values
- how subroutines may declare their own variables, called local variables, and that local variables usually:
  - only exist while the subroutine is executing
  - are only accessible within the subroutine
- how to use local variables and why it is good practice to do so.

3.2.11 Structured programming

- Structured programming is sometimes also called **modular** programming.
- It is important that structured programming uses clear, well-documented interfaces such as local variables and parameters alongside clearly defined **return values.**
- Defined functions are coded in a separate module. This means that modules can be reused in other programs.
- After a module has been tested individually, it is then **integrated** with other modules into the overall program structure. Structured programs use looping constructs such as 'for', 'until' and 'while'.
- Each basic subroutine of a program should perform a simple task.
- A **subtask** could require a single unit or a combination of units.
- Generally speaking, a function returns a value and can be included within an **expression**, but a procedure does not.

> **Exam tip**
>
> 'Arguments' and 'parameters' are sometimes used, but AQA use the term 'parameter' to refer to both of these.

Benefits of modular programming

REVISED

- It makes the coding so much easier.
- Once written, modules can be **checked individually** and then be placed in the correct order within the program.
- Some tasks are quite generic, for example you may need to perform a particular mathematical operation within your code.
- To avoid unnecessary work, all programming languages have **predefined** modules that can be called. It is possible to 'call' any module.
- When a module is called, the name for this is a **subroutine** or **procedure**.
- A procedure is a special kind of module that performs a task or set of tasks that can be added to another program as a subtask of that particular program.

AQA pseudo-code for modular programming

REVISED

Subroutine definition

```
SUBROUTINE Identifier(parameters)
    <statements here>
ENDSUBROUTINE
```

> **Example**
> ```
> SUBROUTINE show_add(a, b)
>     result ← a + b
>     OUTPUT result
> ENDSUBROUTINE
> SUBROUTINE say_hi()
>     OUTPUT 'hi'
> ENDSUBROUTINE
> ```

Subroutine return value

```
RETURN Exp
```

Example

```
SUBROUTINE add(a, b)
    result ← a + b
    RETURN result
ENDSUBROUTINE
```

Calling a subroutine

```
Identifier(parameters)
```

Example

```
show_add(2, 3)
answer ← add(2, 3)
```

Exam practice

1 State the THREE different structured programming constructs. [3]

2 Briefly describe the term 'module'. [2]

3 What is structured programming? [2]

4 Give TWO characteristics of structured programming. [2]

5 Give TWO advantages of structured programming. [2]

6 State the FOUR main advantages of structured programming. [4]

7 What is a structure? [1]

8 What is meant by an array of structures? [1]

Answers can be found on pages 138–9

Summary

You should now have an understanding of:
● the structured approach to programming
● the structured approach including modularised programming, clear, well-documented interfaces (local variables, parameters) and return values
● the advantages of the structured approach.

3.2.12 Robust and secure programming

Data validation

- The following **validation** checks are examples of simple data validation routines:
  - ○ checking if an entered string has a minimum length
  - ○ checking if a string is empty
  - ○ checking if data entered lies within a given range (e.g. between 1 and 10).
- Validation is an automatic check performed by a computer to ensure that entered data is **sensible/feasible**.
- It does not check the **accuracy** of the data entered.

Why use validation?

- A program could crash if the incorrect data is input by a **user**.
- The code may also produce incorrect results when processing the data.

The most common validation checks are:

Type of check	Explanation
Length check	Checks than an entered data value is no longer than a set number of characters. For example, checks the data isn't too long or too short.
Presence check	Checks that some data has been entered into a field.
Range check	For example, a user of a computer system is likely to be aged between 3 and 110. The computer can be programmed only to accept numbers between 3 and 110. However, this does not guarantee that the number typed in is correct. For example, the user could be 5 years of age but say that they are 16.
Type check	Checks that the value of data is of a particular type, for example that age data is numeric.
Format check	A format check is more advanced than a type check, for example, it can be used to check a postcode format.

There are a number of other validation types that can be used to check the data that is being entered.
- Cardinality check: checks that record has a valid number of related records.
- Check digit: the last one or two digits in any code are used to check the other digits are correct.
- Consistency check: checks fields to ensure data in these fields corresponds, for example, If Title = 'Mr.', then Gender = 'M'.
- Spell check: looks up words in a dictionary or array.

Validating the presence of data

One common error is no data in a field where data is required. For example, id is frequently required as is name. A pseudo-code example testing for the **presence** of a name is shown below:

```
IF LEN(name)=0 THEN:    # spaces is a variable set when
                        # the string = 0 char
    OUTPUT "missing name"
    invalid ← TRUE
ENDIF
```

Validating data type

Often non-numeric data is put into a numeric field. However you can validate for character data in a character field. Assume that myNumber is a **numeric** field and you want to make sure that no non-numeric data is entered in the field.

```
Invalid ← FALSE
IF NOT is_numeric (myNumber) THEN
    OUTPUT "non-numeric data in myNumber"
    invalid ← TRUE
ENDIF
```

Range checks

We can use similar code for a range check. Say we want to limit the maximum age someone can enter:

```
input = input("Please provide your age: ")
input = int(input)          # we must convert the
                            # user input to an integer

if input > 120:
    print ("Error! You cannot be that old!")
```

Or the minimum age:

```
input = input("Please provide your age: ")
input = int(input)
if input < 6:
    print ("Error! You cannot be that young!")
```

Errors

There are basically three types of error that computer programmers encounter when writing code. These are:
● syntax errors
● runtime errors
● logic errors.

Syntax errors

● A syntax error occurs when the programmer fails to obey one of the grammar rules of the programming language they are writing their application in.
● Whilst syntax errors usually prevent the program from running in some way, they are not easily found by a human.
● Typically, syntax errors are down to using the wrong case, placing punctuation in positions where it should not exist or failing to insert punctuation where it should be placed within the code.

The most common syntax errors are when the programmer forgets to put:
● the quotes around a string.
● a colon at the end of an if, elif, else, for, while, class, or def statement.

Name errors

You may also have a name error.

This happens when you have:
- misspelt a variable, function or method name
- forgotten to import a module
- forgotten to define a variable.

You will need to be able to find errors in both your own code and the examination code so you will need to understand how to do this.

Logic errors

- Out of the three common errors that occur in programming, logic errors are typically the most difficult kind of errors to detect and rectify.
- This is usually because there is no obvious indication of the error within the software.
- The code will run successfully but it will not behave in the way it was designed to. In other words, it will simply produce incorrect results.

The most common reasons for logic errors are:
- The programmer did not understand the manner in which the program was meant to behave.
- The programmer did not understand the individual behaviour of each operation that was part of the program.
- Careless programming.

Runtime errors

A runtime error is an error that does not show itself until the program runs on the machine it is intended for. Good examples of this are when a program runs out of memory or when a website uses html code that is not compatible with the web browser being used, as these both often cause runtime errors.

Testing

There are three types of test data.

Under normal conditions:
- The application is tested under normal working conditions and the coded solution is supplied with data that is within the anticipated range.

Under extreme conditions:
- The coded solution is provided with data that is within the operating range but at its limits of performance.

Under erroneous conditions:
- With tests under erroneous conditions, an application or program is provided with data that is outside of its limits of performance. These particular tests try to break the application and to investigate if things occur when they shouldn't or vice versa.

Trace tables

A trace table is a technique used to test algorithms to see if any logic errors are occurring whilst the algorithm is being processed. Within the table, each column contains a variable, and each row displays each numerical input into the algorithm and the resultant values of the variables.

```
1 y = 2          # variable y = 2
2 x = 2          # variable x = 2
3 y = y + x
```

Line	y	x
1	2	
2	2	2
3	4	2

Exam practice

1 What are the THREE types of error that computer programmers encounter when writing software?   [3]

2 What is meant by a format error and what is its correct name?   [4]

3 State what happens when programming statements are written in the wrong order, also stating the name for this type of error.   [3]

4 Which type of programming error is the hardest to detect and why?   [3]

5 What is the name given to the testing of software at the planning and flowchart stage?   [2]

6 What is a trace table?   [3]

7 What is correcting errors in a program called?   [1]
   A   compiling
   B   debugging
   C   grinding
   D   interpreting

Answers can be found on page 139

Summary

You should now have an understanding of:
- how to write simple data validation routines
- how to use data validation techniques to write simple routines that check the validity of data being entered by a user
- how to write simple authentication routines
- how to write a simple authentication routine that uses a username and password. Students will only be required to use plain-text usernames and passwords (i.e. students will not need to encrypt the passwords)
- how to select suitable test data that covers normal (typical), boundary (extreme) and erroneous data
- how to justify the choice of test data.

3.2.13 Classification of programming languages

Computer languages

Computer languages are classified as:
- high-level languages
- low-level languages
- assembly language
- machine language (referred to as **machine code**).

Why different languages?

The high-level languages are much closer to human language than low-level languages.

But a high-level language must use an **interpreter**, **compiler** or **translator** to convert a human-understandable program into a computer-readable language called machine code.

Advantages of low-level languages

- If a programmer writes code in a low-level language it does not require **translation**.
- A low-level language does not need a **compiler** or **interpreter** to run; the processor for which the language was written is able to run the code without needing to translate the code into something it understands.

Advantages of high-level languages

- **Debugging** is easier in a high-level language.
- High-level programming techniques are applicable everywhere, even where computational resources are limited.
- High-level languages make complex programming simpler.
- Humans create fewer **errors** in high-level languages.
- The length of the program is small compared with low-level languages.
- The main advantage of high-level languages over low-level languages is that they are easier for humans to read, write and **maintain**.
- Unlike with low-level languages the programmer does not need detailed knowledge of a particular internal computer architecture.

Assembly language

- Assembly language is a good example of a low-level language.
- Assembly language is at the level of telling the processor what to do.
- It is between machine languages and high-level languages.
- The word 'low' refers to the small or non-existent amount of **abstraction** between the language used and machine code.
- A low-level language does not need a compiler or interpreter to run the program.
- Assembly language has the same structure and set of commands as machine language, but it enables a programmer to use names instead of numbers.
- Assembly language uses mnemonic codes for instructions and allows the programmer to introduce names for blocks of memory that hold data.
- Assembly language is designed to be easily translated into machine language.

> **Exam tip**
>
> Like machine language, assembly language requires detailed knowledge of a particular internal computer architecture.

Machine language/code

Machine code or machine language is a system of instructions and data executed directly by a computer's **CPU**.

- It is the lowest-level programming language.
- It is a set of instructions in binary that is used to represent operations and data in a machine.
- It is a collection of binary digits, or bits, that the computer reads and interprets.
- It is directly executable by a computer without the need for translation by a compiler or an assembler.
- It is the native language of the computer.

Conversion from high-level language to low-level language

Translators are just computer programs which accept a program written in a high-level or low-level language and produce an equivalent machine-level program as output.

A translator is a computer program that translates one programming language instruction into another programming language instruction.

A computer source code is to be translated into a low-level programming language where native code compilers change it into machine language for execution.

Translators are of one of three types:
- assembler
- compiler
- interpreter.

> **Exam tip**
>
> If you don't have time to write sentences, but you do know what to do, then just write bullet points.

Assembler

- An assembler **converts** assembly language's source code into machine language.
- It is a program that takes high-level language and converts it into a pattern of bits (0s and 1s) that the computer runs to produce results.

Compiler

- A compiler is a program that compiles **source code** into executable instructions that a computer can understand. It compiles code and produces it in a new format **before** it runs.

Interpreter

- An interpreter is a program that **executes** programming code directly.
- Interpreters can convert source code using a step-by-step, line-by-line and unit-by-unit basis into machine code.
- Interpreted languages are therefore read and executed directly, with no compilation stage.

Interpreter	Compiler
It converts the program into machine code one statement at a time or calls a routine in its own code to execute the command.	It converts all the code of the program into machine code at the same time.
It takes less time to analyse the source code, but the overall program execution time is slower.	The first time the program is run it takes a large amount of time to analyse the source code, but once the compilation has taken place there is no need for any translation on subsequent runs of the program.
A client buying the software would need the translator software.	A client buying the software would not need the translator software.
It continues translating the program until the first error is met, in which case it stops.	It generates error messages after searching for all the errors of a program and then lists them.

Exam practice

1 Which of the statements below is valid about an interpreter?   [1]
   A   it translates one instruction at a time
   B   object code is saved for future use
   C   repeated interpretation is not necessary
   D   all of the above

2 The translator program used in assembly language is called a/an ...   [1]
   A   compiler   B   interpreter   C   assembler   D   translator

3 A computer program that converts an entire program into machine language is called a/an ...   [1]
   A   interpreter   B   simulator   C   compiler   D   commander

4 What is a compiler?   [1]
   A   a compiler does a conversion line by line as the program is run
   B   a compiler converts the whole of a high-level program code into machine code in one step
   C   a compiler is a general purpose language providing very efficient execution
   D   none of the above

5 A compiler translates a program written in a high-level language into ...   [1]
   A   machine language   C   a debugged program
   B   an algorithm   D   none of these

Answers can be found on page 139

Summary

You should now have an understanding of:
- different levels of programming language:
  - low-level language
  - high-level language
- why most computer programs are written in high-level languages
- the main differences between low-level and high-level languages
- how machine code and assembly language are considered to be low-level languages and the differences between them
- how processors execute machine code and that each type of processor has its own specific machine code instruction set
- how assembly language is often used to develop software for embedded systems and for controlling specific hardware components
- how assembly language has a 1:1 correspondence with machine code
- how ultimately all programming code written in high-level or assembly languages must be translated into machine code
- how machine code is expressed in binary and is specific to a processor or family of processors
- the advantages and disadvantages of low-level language programming compared with high-level language programming
- the three common types of program translator:
  - interpreter
  - compiler
  - assembler
- the main differences between these three types of translator
- when it would be appropriate to use each type of translator.

Both Papers

3.3 Fundamentals of data representation

3.3.1 Number bases

Understanding number bases

We usually write numbers in **base 10**, using the symbols 0, 1, 2, 3, 4, 5, 6, 7, 8 and 9. For example, 71 means seven 10s and one unit. However numbers can be written in any number base.

Base two, called **binary**, is particularly useful in electronic circuits because it only requires two symbols, for zero and one; this is the way numbers are represented in computers as a switch can be on or off.

Just as in base 10, the columns represent powers of 10 and have 'place value' 1, 10, 10^2, 10^3 etc. (reading from right to left), so in base 2, the columns represent powers of 2. Hence the number 1001011 denotes (reading from right to left):

one unit (2^0), one two (2^1), no fours (2^2), one eight (2^3), no 16 (2^4), no 32 (2^5), one 64 (2^6).

The number 1001011 in base 2 is the same as the number 75 in base 10.

Working with computers you will also encounter base 16 numbers, called **hexadecimal**.

In **hexadecimal** maths, the columns stand for multiples of 16! That is, the first column stands for how many units you have, the second column stands for how many 16, the third column stands for how many 256s (16^2), and so on.

> **Exam tip**
>
> The following equivalent maximum values are used by AQA:
> - decimal: 255
> - binary: 1111 1111
> - hexadecimal: FF

Binary code

Everything a computer does is based on ones and zeros. 1 means 'on' and 0 means 'off'.

On   On   Off   On   Off   Off

- Rather than giving a light just one value, we give the different lights in the sequence different values.
- The value of the first light is 32, the second is 16, then 8, 4, 2, 1.
- The value of those six bulbs (called a point value) would be 32 + 16 + 0 + 4 + 0 + 0 (remember, we only give points if they're turned on!) And that adds up to 52.
- So, we would say the sequence of lights is worth 52.
- But we would write it in binary as 110100.

Converting to binary numbers

Converting decimal numbers to binary numbers is relatively simple.

Decimal number	How we convert	Binary number
0	We start at 0 for the number of bits required. Here we have 7 bits.	0000000
1	Then we add a 1 on the right.	0000001
2	As we already have a 1 at the right it changes back to 0 again, but we carry a 1 one place in.	0000010
3	Now we add a 1 on the right again as it is a 0.	0000011
4	We add 1 to the number on the right but that digit is already at 1 so it goes back to 0 and 1 is added to the *next position* on the left, but it is also a 1 so it becomes a zero and we carry the 1 one place to the left.	0000**100**
5	Now we add a 1 on the right again as it is a 0.	0000101
6	As we want to add a 1 to the right and it is already a 1 we make it a 0 and put the 1 up one place to the left.	0000**110**
7	Now we add a 1 on the right again as it is a 0.	0000111
8	Start back at 0 again (for all three digits), and a 1 is carried to the left.	0001000
9	And so on ...	0001001

To **convert** from decimal numbers to binary we divide the number successively by 2 and print the remainder in reverse order.

So, if we have a **decimal** number of 51 we can work out its binary equivalent as follows:

Number divided by 2		Remainder
51/2	25	1
25/2	12	1
12/2	6	0
6/2	3	0
3/2	1	1
1/2	0	1

Answer: 110011

Adding binary numbers

REVISED

Adding binary numbers is relatively simple.

$0 + 0 = 0$

$1 + 0 = 1$

$0 + 1 = 1$

$1 + 1 = 0$ carry 1

$1 + 1 + 1 = 1$ carry 1

Adding together three rows works the same way.

Binary shift

REVISED

If we **shift** the decimal point in a decimal number to the right it multiplies the number by 10, but in binary it multiplies the number by only 2.

Hexadecimal numbers

REVISED

Computers can use hexadecimal numbers. There are 16 hexadecimal digits.

Hexadecimal numbers are the same as decimal up to 9.

Decimal	0	1	2	3	4	5	6	7
Hexadecimal	0	1	2	3	4	5	6	7
Binary	0000	0001	0010	0011	0100	0101	0110	0111

Decimal	8	9	10	11	12	13	14	15
Hexadecimal	8	9	A	B	C	D	E	F
Binary	1000	1001	1010	1011	1100	1101	1110	1111

Decimal to hexadecimal

REVISED

Converting decimal numbers to hexadecimal numbers is much harder than converting decimals to binary numbers. We always work backwards to convert these numbers.

So, if we have the **decimal** number 1128 we can work out its hexadecimal equivalent as follows:

What to do	Division	Integer	Remainder (in hexadecimal)
Start by dividing the number by 16, that is 1128/16. 1128 divided by 16 is 70.5. So the integer division result is 70, record this in the Integer column. The remainder is (70.5 – 70) is 0.5. This is then multiplied by 16, giving a result of 8. Record this in the Remainder column.	1128/16	70	8
Now divide the result number by 16: 70/16. 70/16 = 4.375. So the integer division result is 4. The remainder, 0.375, is multiplied by 16, which is 6.	70/16	4	6
The next stage is 4/16 = 0.25. The integer division result is 0. The remainder, 0.25, is multiplied by 16, which is 4.	4/16	0	4
Stop because the result is already 0 (0 divided by 16 will always be 0).			
We now have the hexadecimal equivalent of the decimal number by working up from the bottom of our remainder column: 468.			

Hexadecimal to decimal

REVISED

So what if the number 1128 was a hexadecimal number and not a decimal number, and we wanted to find its decimal equivalent? This would be calculated as follows:

The last number is 8. It represents $8 \times (16^0)$ which equals 8

The next number is 2. This represents $2 \times (16^1) = 32$

The next number is 1. This will be $1 \times (16^2) = 256$

And lastly $1 \times (16^3) = 4096$

If we add the totals together 1128 in hexadecimal = 4392 in denary (decimal).

> **Exam tip**
>
> If you are running out of time and have two questions left to do, the way to maximise your marks is to do the first half of both of them.

Exam practice

1 A number system that has two different symbols to represent any quantity is known as ...   [1]
   A   binary
   B   octal
   C   decimal
   D   hexadecimal

2 A number system that has ten different symbols to represent any quantity is known as ...   [1]
   A   binary
   B   octal
   C   decimal
   D   hexadecimal

3 A number system that has eight different symbols to represent any quantity is known as ... [1]
   A binary
   B octal
   C decimal
   D hexadecimal

4 A number system that has 16 different symbols to represent any quantity is known as ... [1]
   A binary
   B octal
   C decimal
   D hexadecimal

5 The least significant bit of a binary number, which is equivalent to any odd decimal number, is ... [1]
   A 0
   B 1
   C 1 or 0
   D 3

Answers can be found on page 139

Summary

You should now have an understanding of:
- the following number bases:
  - decimal (base 10)
  - binary (base 2)
  - hexadecimal (base 16)
- how binary can be used to represent whole numbers
- how decimal values between 0 and 255 are represented in binary
- how hexadecimal can be used to represent whole numbers
- how decimal values between 0 and 255 are represented in hexadecimal
- how to convert in both directions between:
  - binary and decimal
  - binary and hexadecimal
  - decimal and hexadecimal.

3.3.3 Units of information

Bit

A **bit** is a value of either a 1 or 0 (on or off). It is the **fundamental** unit of information.

Nibble

A **nibble** is 4 bits.

Byte

A **byte** is group of 8 bits.

Quantities of bytes can be described using prefixes:
- kilo, 1 kB is 1,000 bytes
- mega, 1 MB is 1,000 kilobytes
- giga, 1 GB is 1,000 megabytes
- tera, 1 TB is 1,000 gigabytes.

Historically the terms 'kilobyte', 'megabyte', etc. have often been used to represent **powers** of 2.

The SI units of kilo, mega and so forth refer to values based on powers of 10. When referring to powers of 2 the terms 'kibi', 'mebi' and so forth would normally be used.

Storage size and data transfer measurements

It is easy to get confused about the difference between kb, kB, Mb, MiB, MB, TB, GB, bytes/s, bits/s.

There is significant difference between **data size** and **data speed**; they are measured differently too.

The difference not only lies in the 'b' (Bit) and 'B' (byte), but also lies on the 'k' and 'K' or the 'm' or 'M' and so forth. Upper-case 'K'/'M' is used in the storage industry and lower-case 'k'/'m' is used in the telecommunications industry.

In **networking** speed is measured in bps ('b' is in lower-case).

Always use the lower-case 'b' in case of networking and data speed handling:
- bits per second OR bits/sec OR bits/s are the other names of bps
- bytes per second OR bytes/sec OR bytes/s are the other names of Bps.

Exam practice

1 One nibble is equal to ...   [1]
  A 1 bit
  B 2 bits
  C 4 bits
  D 8 bits

2 The word length of a Personal Computer is ...   [1]
  A 4 bits
  B 8 bits
  C 16 bits
  D 64 bits

3 Which statement is valid?   [1]
  A 1 KB = 1,024 bytes
  B 1 MB = 2,048 bytes
  C 1 MB = 1,000 kilobytes
  D 1 KB = 1,000 bytes

4 Bit stands for ...   [1]
  A binary digits
  B bits of a system
  C part of a byte
  D all of the above

5 A byte consists of ...   [1]
  A one bit
  B four bits
  C eight bits
  D sixteen bits

6 1 kilobyte refers to ...   [1]
  A 1,000 bytes
  B 1,024 bytes
  C 8,000 bytes
  D 8,192 bytes

7 The term 'gigabyte' refers to ...   [1]
  A 1,000 bytes
  B 1,000 kilobytes
  C 1,000 megabytes
  D 1,000 gigabyte

8 Which is the largest?   [1]
  A 1 kilobyte
  B 1 petabyte
  C 1 terabyte
  D 1 gigabyte

Answers can be found on page 139

Summary

You should now have an understanding of:
- units:
  - a bit is the fundamental unit of information
  - a byte is a group of 8 bits
  - a bit is either a 0 or a 1
  - b represents bit
  - B represents byte
- how quantities of bytes can be described using prefixes
- the names, symbols and corresponding values for the decimal prefixes:
  - kilo, 1 kB is 1,000 bytes
  - mega, 1 MB is 1,000 kilobytes
  - giga, 1 GB is 1,000 megabytes
  - tera, 1 TB is 1,000 gigabytes.

3.3.4 Binary arithmetic

Adding binary numbers

Adding binary numbers is relatively simple. You first align the numbers you wish to add as you would if you were adding decimal numbers.

```
0  1  1  1
1  1  1  0
```

You then add the two numbers in the far right column, again as you would decimal numbers.

```
0  1  1  1
1  1  1  0
_____
            1
```

Add the numbers following the rules of binary addition (1 + 0 = 1, 0 + 0 = 0) unless both numbers are a 1. If they are both 1, write 0 below and carry a 1 to the next column. (Remember it is not 'ten' but 'one zero'.)

```
0  1  1  1
1  1  1  0
_____
         0  1
```

Move on to the next column to the left. We use the rule 1 + 1 + 1 = 1 carry 1.

```
0  1  1  1
1  1  1  0
_____
      1  0  1
```

We start on the right and move across the columns to the left. If there are no more columns, we add a new one.

```
   0  1  1  1
   1  1  1  0
_____
1  0  1  0  1
```

Remember that 1 + 1 = 10 and 1 + 1 + 1 = 11. Always remember to carry the 1. If we want to add three binary numbers this is achieved in exactly the same way. When we add three numbers the rule is that 1 + 1 + 1 + carry 1 = 1 0 0.

```
   1  1  0  1
   1  0  1  1
   1  1  0  1
_____
1  0  0  1  0  1
```

Add rightmost column = 1 + 1 + 1 so we have 1 and need to also carry 1 to the next column.

Add the next column = 0 + 1 + 0 but we also have the 1 carried so 0 and we carry 1 again to the next column.

Add the next column 1 + 0 + 1 + the 1 that was carried so the answer is 1 with the carry of 1.

In the fourth column we have 1 + 1 + 1 with a carry of 1 as well. Adding four 1s results in a 0 in this column with a 1 carried two columns to the left. Two new columns need to be created for the 1 to be carried across by two columns. The answer is 100101

Binary shifts

If we shift the decimal point in a decimal number to the right it multiplies the number by 10. So 1.2 would become 12. If we move the point two places it would become 120. This is because we use a 10-unit numbering system. Binary uses a 2-unit system and therefore a shift one place to the right in a binary number is the same as multiplying by 2.

Moving the decimal point to the right is the same as moving the digits to the left.

Binary shifts can be used to perform simple multiplication/division by powers of 2.

Shifting the digits left one place is the same as multiplying by 2.

Decimal	128	64	32	16	8	4	2	1
Input	0	0	1	0	0	1	0	1
Result	0	1	0	0	1	0	1	0

> **Exam tip**
>
> Read the questions carefully.

A left shift of two places is the same as multiplying by 4.

Decimal	128	64	32	16	8	4	2	1
Input	0	0	1	0	0	1	0	1
Result	1	0	0	1	0	1	0	0

A left shift of three places is the same as multiplying by 8.

Decimal	256	128	64	32	16	8	4	2	1
Input	0	0	0	1	0	0	1	0	1
Result	1	0	0	1	0	1	0	0	0

In general shifting N places left is the same as multiplying by 2 to the power N (written as 2^N).

If we shift to the right one place this is the same as dividing by 2.

Decimal	256	128	64	32	16	8	4	2	1
Input	0	0	1	0	0	1	0	1	0
Result	0	0	0	1	0	0	1	0	1

Exam practice

1 Complete the binary addition chart. One has been done for you.
Your answer should be shown as an 8-bit number.   [4]

Addition	Answer
101 + 11 =	00001000
111 + 111 =	
1010 + 1010 =	
11101 + 1010 =	
11111 + 11111 =	

Answers can be found on page 139

Summary

You should now have an understanding of:
- how to add together up to three binary numbers
  You will be expected to use a maximum of 8 bits and a maximum
  of three values to add and answers will be a maximum of 8 bits in
  length and will not involve carrying beyond the 8 bits.
- how to apply a binary shift to a binary number
  You will be expected to use a maximum of 8 bits.
  You will be expected to understand and use only a logical binary shift.
  You will not need to understand or use fractional representations.
- situations where binary shifts can be used.

3.3.5 Character encoding

ASCII

- **ASCII** stands for American Standard Code for Information Interchange.
- Computers can only understand numbers, so an ASCII code is the **numerical** representation of characters such from 'a' to 'z', '@' or even an action of some sort.
- The original ASCII only uses 7-bit numbers to represent the letters, numerals and common punctuation used in the English language.
- As there are two possibilities per bit, we have $2^7 = 128$ possible values it can represent, from 0 to 127 inclusive. Remember, 0 is also a reference so we have 128 possible values to store our characters.

Each of those 128 values is **assigned** to a character.

	0000	0001	0010	0011	0100	0101	0110	0111
0000	NULL	DLE		0	@	P	`	P
0001	SOH	DC1	!	1	A	Q	a	q
0010	STX	DC2	"	2	B	R	b	r
0011	ETX	DC3	#	3	C	S	c	s
0100	EDT	DC4	$	4	D	T	d	t
0101	ENQ	NAK	%	5	E	U	e	u
0110	ACK	SYN	&	6	F	V	f	v
0111	BEL	ETB	'	7	G	W	g	w
1000	BS	CAN	(	8	H	X	h	x
1001	HT	EM	)	9	I	Y	i	y
1010	LF	SUB	*	:	J	Z	j	z
1011	VT	ESC	+	;	K	[	k	{
1100	FF	FS	,	<	L	\	l	|
1101	GR	GS	-	=	M	]	m	}
1110	SO	RS	.	>	N	^	n	~
1111	SI	US	/	?	O	_	o	DEL

- For example, in ASCII the number 65 represents an upper-case letter 'A' and 61 represents an equals sign. So if the output sent to a display receives an ASCII value of 65, it displays an upper-case letter A on the screen.
- There is no real reason that A has to be character number 65, that's just the number the developers working on telegraph systems chose when ASCII was first developed.
- In ASCII, codes run sequentially so ASCII 'A' is coded as 65, 'B' as 66, and so on, meaning that the codes for the other upper-case letters can be calculated once the code for 'A' is known. This pattern also applies to other groupings such as lower-case letters and digits.

If we wanted to translate 'Hello' into ASCII it would look like this:

ASCII	01001000	01100101	01101100	01101100	1101111
Text	H	e	l	l	o

Extended ASCII

- ASCII works fine for English strings such as 'Hello World', but suppose we want to store a German string such as: 'Es gefällt mir nicht' (translates as: 'I do not like it').
- It was decided that as ASCII had an extra bit which was not in use, if ASCII was made into a 8-bit code rather than 7, it could store another 128 values. This system is called **extended ASCII**.
- The problem was that different groups used the same initial ASCII characters, but came up with different extended ASCII character set numbers. For example, in the Western Europe extended ASCII **character set**, number 224 represents a lower-case letter A with a grave accent. But in Eastern Europe the same number represents a lower-case letter R with an acute accent. Added to this, a 256-character set is no use in languages like Chinese and Japanese, where there are literally thousands of characters in common use.

The Unicode character set

- Although originally designed for 16 bits, the latest version of **Unicode** stores each character with 32 bits. Unicode can also use 8 bits. It presently contains over 110,000 characters and has space for 1,114,111 different values that can be used for characters, so at present only around 10% are used.
- Unicode uses the same codes as ASCII up to 127.
- The chart shows just a few of the foreign language characters supported.

Code (hex)	Character	Source
0041	A	English (Latin)
042F	Я	Russian (Cyrillic)
262F	☯	Symbols
03A3	Σ	Greek
211E	℞	Letterlike symbol
21CC	⇌	Arrows
28FF	⣿	Braille
2EDD	食	Chinese/Japanese/Korean (Common)

Exam practice

1 What does ASCII stand for? [1]
   A American Standard Code for Information Interchange
   B American Scientific Code for International Interchange
   C American Standard Code for Intelligence Interchange
   D American Scientific Code for Information Interchange

2 The original ASCII code used ___ bits of each byte, reserving the last bit for error checking. [1]
   A 5
   B 6
   C 7
   D 8

3 What will the following pseudo-code do? [1]

```
CHAR_TO_CODE('a')
```

4 What will the following pseudo-code do?   [1]

    CODE_TO_CHAR(97)

5 What is the commonly used standard data code to represent
   alphabetical, numerical and punctuation characters used in
   electronic data processing system called?   [1]
   A   ASCII
   B   ASCIII
   C   high-level language
   D   low-level language

6 What is the difference between ASCII and Extended ASCII?   [2]

7 What are the main advantages of UNICODE over ASCII?   [4]

Answers can be found on page 139

Summary

You should now have an understanding of:
- what a character set is and these character encoding methods:
  - 7-bit ASCII
  - Unicode
- how to use a given character encoding table to convert:
  - characters to character codes
  - character codes to characters
- how character codes are commonly grouped and run in sequence
  within encoding tables
- the purpose of Unicode and the advantages of Unicode over ASCII
- the need for data representation of different alphabets and of
  special symbols allowing a far greater range of characters.

3.3.6 Representing images

Bitmaps

A bitmap image stores each individual **pixel**.

First you need to understand black and white images. 0 is stored for a white pixel, 1 is stored for a black pixel. Each black and white pixel takes up 1 bit of storage.

An example would be:

0	0	1	1	1	1	0	0
0	1	0	0	0	0	1	0
0	1	0	0	0	0	1	0
1	0	1	0	0	1	0	1
0	1	0	0	0	0	1	0
0	1	0	1	1	0	1	0
0	0	1	0	0	1	0	0
0	0	0	1	1	0	0	0

This would create the following image:

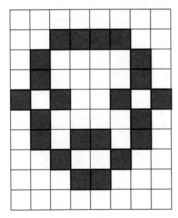

Resolution

Resolution is the name we use for the **number of pixels** that the image takes up. It relates to the number of pixels displayed on the screen.

With a **higher resolution** we have a clearer and more detailed picture but we use more pixels – hence the image takes up more memory.

Black and white image size

A **greyscale** (black and white) image uses one byte per pixel (a byte being 8 bits). A byte can store up to 256 different values. We can therefore store up to 256 levels of brightness per pixel – which gives us an '8-bit greyscale'.

Calculating storage requirements

If we need to calculate the storage requirements of a black and white bitmap image we multiply the **number of pixels wide** by the **number of pixels high**. This answer will give us the number of **bits**.

We then convert the number into an appropriate unit (kilobytes/megabytes).

Example:

A black and white image is 800 pixels by 900 pixels. Calculate the storage requirements and express the answer in appropriate units.

Step 1: Length × Width

$800 × 900 = 720,000$ bits

Step 2: Convert into appropriate units

$720,000/8 = 90,000$ bytes

$90,000/1,000 = 90$ kB

VDUs display pictures by dividing the display screen into thousands (or millions) of pixels, arranged into rows and columns.

The size of an image is expressed directly as width of image in pixels by height of image in pixels using the notation width × height.

Colour depth is the number of bits used to represent each pixel.

Size in bits = W × H × D

Size in bytes = W × H × D / 8

where W = image width

H = image height

D = colour depth in bits.

Exam tip

You will only need to use colour depth and number of pixels within your calculations.

Exam practice

1 Describe the differences between digital and analogue data. [6]

2 Which of the following requires a large amount of a computer's memory? [1]
   A   imaging
   B   graphics
   C   voice
   D   all of the above

3 A true colour image is 800 pixels by 900 pixels. It uses 24 bits for three RGB colours. Calculate the storage requirements and express the answer in appropriate units. [6]

4 You take a digital photograph which is 800 pixels by 600 pixels. Each pixel has its own red, green, and blue values stored in 1 byte. How many bytes are required to store the whole image in RAM and how would this differ on a hard drive where it is stored as a jpg file? [5]

Answers can be found on page 140

Summary

You should now have an understanding of:

● what a pixel is and how pixels relate to an image and the way images are displayed
● the term 'pixel' being short for picture element; a pixel being a single point in a graphical image
● the following for bitmaps:
    – size in pixels
    – colour depth
● how a bitmap represents an image using pixels and colour depth
● how bitmaps are made from pixels
● how the number of pixels and colour depth can affect the file size of a bitmap image
● how higher numbers of pixels and higher colour depths can affect file size and should also be able to use examples
● how to calculate bitmap image file sizes based on the number of pixels and colour depth
● how to convert binary data into a black and white image.

Given a binary pattern that represents a black and white bitmap, you should be able to draw the resulting image as a series of pixels.

You must be able to convert a black and white image into binary data.

Given a black and white bitmap, you should be able to write down a bit pattern that represents the image.

3.3.7 Representing sound

Sound

- Original sound is in **analogue** form, it's how our ears work. But to turn this sound into something a computer can handle we need to create a digital sound wave.

Original analogue sound wave

Digitised sound wave

- In analogue recording, the machine is **constantly** recording any sound or noise that is coming through the microphones. In digital recording, you don't have a constant recording, you have a series of **samples** or snapshots which are a measure of amplitude at a given point in time and are taken from the sound being recorded.

Analogue to digital converter

An analogue to digital **converter** constantly measures the amplitude (volume) of an incoming electrical voltage from a microphone or sound source.

It then outputs these measurements as a long list of binary bytes, for example
10110100101000101001001001001010101010101

Sampling rate is the number of samples taken in a second and is usually measured in **hertz** (1 hertz = 1 sample per second).

Sample **resolution** is the number of bits per sample.

File size (bits) = rate × res × secs   rate = sampling rate

where res = sample resolution

secs = number of seconds.

Given a bitmap representation and you will be expected to show the frequency and value pairs for each row, for example
0000011100000011 would become 5 0 3 1 6 0 2 1.

Bit depth

- Bit **depth** defines the dynamic range of the sound – the amplitude (volume) of the waveform at each sample point.
- **Quantisation** is the name of the audio 'snapshot' when it has to be rounded off to the nearest available digital value.
- Sample rates are measured in hertz (Hz) or thousands of hertz (kHz – kilohertz). For example, 44.1 kHz is equal to 44,100 samples of audio recorded every second. The sample rate you choose depends on what the audio is going to be used for. If you wanted to record a song to put onto CD you would usually use 44.1 kHz.

Calculating file sizes

We can calculate sound file sizes based on the **sampling** rate and the sample resolution using the following formula:

File size (bits) = rate × res × secs = sampling rate

If we want 30 seconds of mono sound, where the sample rate is 44,100 and the sample resolution is 8 bits, we will have:

File size = (44,100 × 8 × 30)/(8 × 1,000)

[divided by 8 as we have 8 bits in a byte and divided by 1,000 to get kHz]

= 1,323 kB

= 1.32 MB

The size of 30 seconds of stereo sound would be: (44,100 × 8 × 2 × 30)/(8 × 1,000)

= 2,646 kB

= 2.6 MB

> **Exam tip**
>
> Leave any questions that you are unsure about to the end.

Bitrate

Digital music files are measured by the amount of information they can play per second. This is usually measured in kbps, or kilobits per second. This is the amount of sound information presented to the listener every second. The bitrate is the number of bits per second.

Sound files played over internet radio are 56 or 64 kbps, to allow faster transport over networks. The standard for near-CD quality is 128 kbps, and some files go up to 320 kbps. If we have a 30-second audio file sampled at a rate of 44.1 kHz and quantised using 8 bits, we can calculate its size by:

bitrate = bitsPerSample × samplesPerSecond × number of channels

To get the file size we would simply multiply the bitrate by the duration (in seconds), and divide by 8 (to get from bits to bytes):

fileSize = (bitsPerSample × samplesPerSecond × channels × duration)/8

Exam practice

1 A microphone is left on for 20 hours recording MP3 audio files. If an MP3 file uses 1 MB in one minute, how much data will that be, expressed in GB? [2]

2 Describe the differences between analogue and digital recordings. [4]

Answers can be found on page 140

Summary

You should now have an understanding of:
● how sound is analogue and that it must be converted to digital form for storage and processing in a computer
● how sound waves are sampled to create the digital version of sound
● how a sample is a measure of amplitude at a point in time
● the digital representation of sound in terms of:
  – sampling rate
  – sample resolution
● how to calculate sound file sizes based on the sampling rate and the sample resolution.

3.3.8 Data compression

- Data **compression** is a set of steps for **packing** data into a smaller 'electronic space' (data bits), while still allowing the original data to be accessed and used.
- This is often achieved by **eliminating** the **repetition** of **identical** sets of data bits (redundancy).
- Compression results in much smaller **storage space** requirements and is often much faster for communications. Compressed data works more effectively on mobile phones and portable computers.

Run-length encoding

REVISED

Run-length encoding (RLE) is a data compression algorithm supported by most **bitmap** file formats, for example TIFF, BMP and PCX.

RLE is suitable for **compressing** any type of data, but the content of the data affects the compression ratio achieved by RLE.

RLE works by reducing the size of a **repeating** string.

A repeating string is called a **run**, and is typically encoded into two bytes:
- the first byte represents the number of characters in the run and is called the run count
- the second byte is the value of the character in the run, which is in the range of 0 to 255, and is called the run value.

Compression with text

REVISED

For an easy-to-understand example of compression with text, we will look at a sentence:

'run-length encoding makes files smaller; smaller files use run-length encoding'

If each character and space in this sentence made up one unit of memory, the whole thing would have a file size of 78 bytes.

There are patterns in our sentence. Most words in the sentence appear twice. Only 'makes' and 'use' appear just once.

But to make use of this pattern we would need to create a **dictionary**, which is simply a way of cataloguing pieces of data, in this case words.

If we created a dictionary using a numbered index to represent each word, it could look something like this:

1 run

2 length

3 encoding

4 makes

5 files

6 smaller

7 use

We could now write the sentence using our numbered index as:
1 2 3 4 5 6; 6 5 7 1 2 3

The compressed file would use **less memory**.

In practice, it will be a little larger as we will need to store our index alongside the data or it will be impossible to read the file, but you will have a good understanding of how this system could work.

Lossless compression

- In lossless **compression**, all original data can be recovered when the file is uncompressed.
- With lossless compression, every bit of data that was originally in the file remains, so nothing is lost when the file is uncompressed.
- The name for this type of algorithm is 'lossless', that is, we lose nothing.

Lossy compression

- If you take a photograph of a country view, large parts of the picture may look the same – the whole sky is blue and the grass is green, for example – but most of the individual pixels are a little bit different.
- The lossless system will not compress the file very well, it could even make the file larger.
- To make this picture smaller without compromising the resolution, you would have to change the colour value for certain pixels to make them the same before compression.
- If the picture had a lot of blue sky, the algorithm could pick one colour of blue that could be used for every pixel and replace all the variations with the same colour. Whilst you will lose the exact information for these different shades of blue and it will never be recoverable (hence lossy compression), most people will not notice a difference.

Huffman encoding

We can also use the **binary tree** to reduce the storage size of text.
- To encode English text, we would need 26 lower-case letters, 26 upper-case letters and some punctuation. Let's say that we could get by with 64 characters.
- We could achieve this with 6 bits but as ASCII uses 7 bits we will also allow up to 7 bits for each character. In text, some characters are more frequent than others.
- We need a system where different characters can be different bit widths, but we also need to tell the system where each character begins and ends without using additional bits for this.

As an example, consider the word ABRACADABRA.

Letter	Frequency
A	5
R	2
B	2
C	1
D	1

We now assign a binary **assignment** to each letter.

Each assignment must be **unique** and easily distinguished from the other assignments. D and C are the least frequent letters used in our word so we will give them the largest assignment of four bits.

As the letter A is the most **frequently** used in our word, we will give it the shortest assignment of one bit.

R and B are the next most frequent so we will give R a two-bit assignment and B an assignment of three bits, as shown in the table.

Letter	Assignment
A	0
R	11
B	100
C	1010
D	1011

Using these assignments we can write ABRACADABRA using our assignments as:

'A'0, 'B'100, 'R'11, 'A'0, 'C'1010, 'A'0, 'D'1011, 'A'0, 'B'100, 'R'11, 'A'0,

which is 01001101010010110100110.

We can find the letters as they have unique assignments. We can find each individual letter easily. This word would now only need 23 bits.

We can then calculate bits saved: 77 − 23 = 54

Let's look at a simple Huffman binary tree and see how we can use it to read the code.

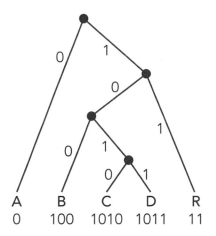

A   B   C   D   R
0   100 1010 1011 11

Looking at the tree, we can work out the word from the code, in 01001101010010110100110, the first 0 can only be an A, a 100 can only be a B, 11 a letter R, etc.

To see how we build the tree in the first place, we will look at how it is constructed. In Huffman coding, we assign bits by creating a binary tree where the **children** are the encoding units with the smallest frequencies.

As you are unlikely to use Huffman coding for a single word, we will examine a sentence with our word inside it.

In practice, many more characters would be used but, as an example of how the system works, we will stay with our five letters and find the assignments for these letters only.

The letter frequencies for our sentence are as follows:

Letter	Frequency
A	40
B	20
R	20
C	10
D	10

The smallest number of occurrences in our sentence are of C and D, so in Huffman coding we must connect these using a binary tree. This creates a new node above C and D which would be called C+D as it is a connection of these two child nodes.

In a binary tree there can only be two nodes. C+D now has a frequency value of 20 as there are 10 Cs and 10 Ds and the **parent** node value will be the two child frequencies added together.

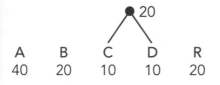

We continue adding our letters until the tree is complete.

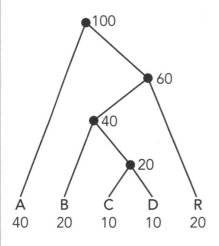

Finally, we assign 0 to all the left branches and 1 to all the right branches.

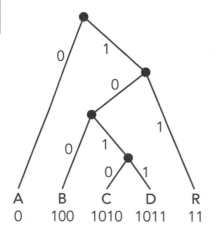

Both papers

Each encoding now shows us a path from the root and each path terminates at a leaf. The path to 'R' is 11, to B is 100. Our assigned values for all the letters are as shown in the table.

Letter	Assignment
A	0
B	100
C	1010
D	1011
R	11

Each is **unique**, so no bit string is a prefix of any other bit string. We have just created an example of Huffman encoding.

Exam practice

1 Explain how compression is achieved with text. In this question you will be marked on your ability to use good English, to organise information clearly and to use specialist vocabulary where appropriate.   [6]

2 Explain what is meant by the term 'run-length encoding'.   [6]

3 Describe what is meant by the term 'data compression'.   [6]

4 Describe the steps required to build an algorithm for a Huffman tree.   [3]

Answers can be found on page 141

Summary

You should now have an understanding of:
- what data compression is
- how common it is for data to be compressed and why it may be necessary or desirable to compress data
- why data may be compressed and there are different ways to compress data
- how data can be compressed using Huffman coding
- how to interpret Huffman trees
- the process of using a tree to represent the Huffman code
- how to interpret a given Huffman tree to determine the code used for a particular node within the tree

- how to calculate the number of bits required to store a piece of data compressed using Huffman coding
- how to calculate the number of bits required to store a piece of uncompressed data in ASCII
- how to carry out calculations to determine the number of bits saved by compressing a piece of data using Huffman coding
- how data can be compressed using run length encoding (RLE)
- the process of using frequency/data pairs to reduce the amount of data stored
- how to represent data in RLE frequency/data pairs.

3.4 Computer systems

3.4.1 Hardware and software 1

The main hardware component parts of a computer

Hardware is the name given to a collection of **physical** 'things' that, when put together in a certain way, form a system.

Processor

- Carries out **computation** and has overall control of the computer.

Main memory

- **Stores** programs and data while the computer is running.
- Is fast access, directly accessible by the processor, limited in size and non-permanent.
- Computers can store data in **main memory** (within the computer itself) or **secondary memory** (backing storage).
- Main memory is any memory device located within the computer system itself and includes:
  - ○ registers (storage within the processor)
  - ○ cache memory (may be in the processor, or just outside it but on the motherboard
  - ○ main memory (mostly RAM, in separate memory chips on the motherboard).

> **Exam tip**
>
> Always stay on topic; if you're discussing the CPU, don't digress and start outlining other hardware.

Secondary memory

- Holds quantities of information too large for storage in main memory.
- Secondary memory is slower access than main memory, not accessible directly by the processor but can be used to keep a permanent copy of programs and data.

External system bus

- This allows communication of information between the component parts of the computer.

Peripheral devices (input/output devices)

● These allow the computer to communicate with the outside world.

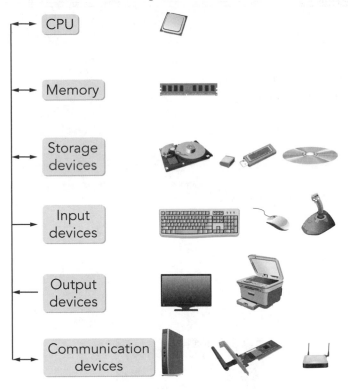

Embedded systems

An **embedded** system is a system that has computer hardware with software embedded in it as one of its components. As embedded systems are small, low cost and simple they have become very popular and are now indispensable in our lives. They are found everywhere, from kitchens to hospitals. Embedded systems:

● frequently have more limited resources than PCs
● usually focus on dedicated tasks, where as PCs are general-purpose computers
● usually require minimal human intervention.

Embedded systems that are being used every day can be found in:

● aircraft (flight landing gear systems and many other systems)
● all gym equipment from treadmills to cycling equipment
● ATMs
● cars (pressure monitoring systems, airbags, power windows and GPS)
● microwave ovens
● military applications
● mobile phones
● pacemakers
● robots
● toys
● TV remotes (and all other remote control devices)
● vending machines
● washing machines (including dishwashers and drying machines)
● and many more …

Actuators and sensors

Micro-processors use **actuators** and **sensors** to function.

Actuators

- An actuator is used to move or control the output.
- It is a type of motor for moving or controlling a mechanism or system.
- To operate, it needs a source of energy, usually in the form of an electric current, hydraulic fluid pressure, or pneumatic pressure.

The **actuator** converts that energy into motion.

Sensors

- A sensor is a converter that measures a physical quantity and converts it into a signal. The micro-controller uses this signal to make a decision.

Micro-controllers need **digital** signals.

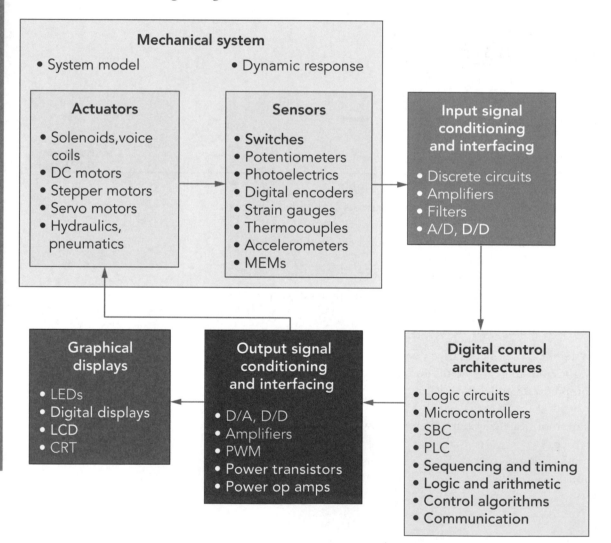

Both papers

Exam practice

1 What is a data bus? [1]

2 What is an address bus? [1]

3 Which of the following is a storage device? [1]
   A Tape
   B Hard disk
   C CD-ROM
   D All of the above

Answers can be found on page 140

Summary

You should now have an understanding of:
- the terms 'hardware' and 'software' and the relationship between them.

3.4.1 Hardware and software 2

Fetch, decode and execute

To **execute** a machine code program it must first be loaded, together with any data that it needs, into main memory (RAM). Once loaded, it is accessible to the CPU which **fetches** one instruction at a time, decodes and executes it.

Fetch, decode and execute are repeated until a program instruction to **HALT** is encountered. This is known as the fetch–execute cycle.

1 **Fetch**
   ○ The instruction is fetched from the memory location whose **address** is contained in the program counter and placed in the instruction register.
   ○ The instruction will consist of an operation code and possibly some operands. The operation code determines which operation is carried out. The term 'opcode' is usually used as a shorthand for operation code.

2 **Decode**
   ○ The pattern of the opcode is **interpreted** by the control unit and the appropriate actions are taken by the electronic circuitry of the CPU.
   ○ These actions may include the fetching of operands for the instruction from memory or from the general purpose registers.

3 **Increment**
   ○ The program **counter** is incremented.
   ○ The size of the increment will depend upon the length of the instruction in the instruction register. For example, for a 3–byte instruction the PC would be incremented by 3.

4 **Execute**
   ○ The instruction in the instruction register is **executed**.
   ○ This may lead to operands being sent to the ALU for arithmetic processing and the return of the result to one of the general purpose registers. When a **HALT** instruction is received then execution of this program ceases.

> **Exam tip**
>
> Always review your answers. Proofread your answers as much as you can to correct any spelling mistakes and add any extra comments you think are worth mentioning.

Exam practice

1 What is the use of the register in a CPU? [2]
2 What is a program counter? [2]
3 The instructions for starting the computer are housed on … [1]
   A random access memory
   B CD-ROM
   C read-only memory chip
   D all of above

4 Secondary storage devices can store data but they cannot perform which of the following? [1]
   A arithmetic operations
   B logic operations
   C fetch operations
   D any of the above

5 Which device can understand the difference between data and programs? [1]
A input device
B output device
C memory
D microprocessor

6 Which of the following is a read-only memory storage device? [1]
A memory stick
B CD-ROM
C hard disk
D none of these

7 The central processing unit (CPU) consists of ... [1]
A input, output and processing
B control unit, primary storage and secondary storage
C control unit, arithmetic-logic unit and primary storage
D control unit, processing and primary storage

8 Which unit converts computer data into human-readable form? [1]
A input unit
B output unit
C ALU
D control unit

9 ALU stands for ... [1]
A Arithmetic Logic Unit
B Array Logic Unit
C Application Logic Unit
D none of the above

Answers can be found on pages 140–1

Summary

You should now have an understanding of:
● the terms 'hardware' and 'software' and the relationship between them.

3.4.2 Boolean logic

Logic gates

- Logic **gates** can be understood better if you think of simple **switches**. Logic functions depend on **binary** bits of information.
- A simple switch is either open or closed.
- The bits could be represented by a yes or a no, or can be ON (conducting) or OFF (not conducting).
- Whatever the two states might be, we will call one of the states a '1' and the other a '0'. It doesn't matter which we call 1 and which we call 0 if we are consistent, but we will call the closed or conducting state of a switch a 1 and the open or non-conducting state a 0.

OR gates

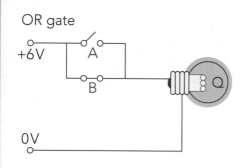

For a two-input OR gate, the output Q is true if EITHER input A 'OR' input B is true, giving the Boolean expression of: (Q = A or B).

We show this in the form of a **truth table**. The truth table specifies the state of the system for each state of the switches:

Inputs		Outputs
A	B	Q
0	0	0
0	1	1
1	0	1
1	1	1

AND gates

We could also look at how a series of switches makes an 'AND' circuit. That is, all switches must be in the '1' state for the system to be in the 1 state (conducting).

For a two-input AND gate, the output Q is true if BOTH input A 'AND' input B are true, giving the Boolean **expression** of: (Q = A and B).

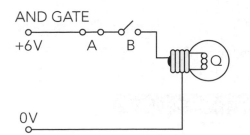

AND GATE

The truth table for the system would look like this:

Inputs		Outputs
A	B	Q
0	0	0
0	1	0
1	0	0
1	1	1

AND yields TRUE only if both values are TRUE:
- FALSE and FALSE = FALSE
- FALSE and TRUE = FALSE
- TRUE and FALSE = FALSE
- TRUE and TRUE = TRUE

NOT gates

REVISED

Unlike AND and OR gates, NOT gates have only one input and one output.

The output is exactly the opposite of the input, so if the input is a 0, the output is a 1 and vice versa.

One input —▷○— One output

NOT is a **unary** operator – it is applied to only one value and inverts it:
- not TRUE = FALSE
- not FALSE = TRUE

1 —▷○— 0   0 —▷○— 1

The truth table would look like this:

Inputs	Outputs
0	1
1	0

Constructing truth tables with more inputs

REVISED

We can easily create a **circuit diagram** from the description of the logic using these symbols. Let's say we want a system where we have four inputs A, B, C and D. We want a circuit that outputs true if either A AND B or C AND D are true.

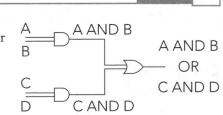

Part of the truth table would look like this:

Inputs				Outputs
A	B	C	D	
1	1	1	0	1
1	1	0	1	1
0	1	0	1	0
1	0	1	0	0
1	1	1	1	1
1	0	1	1	1
0	1	1	1	1

Exam practice

1 If the tyre is flat then I will have to remove the wheel and take it to the garage.

Complete the truth table below to represent each basic statement. [5]

The tyre is flat.	The wheel has been removed.	Take the wheel to the garage.
	1	
1	0	
0	1	
0		

2 Annotate the circuit diagram to show the Boolean outputs. Part of the diagram has been completed for you. [2]

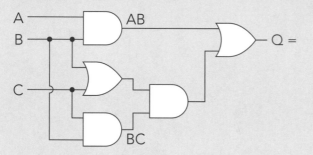

3 Complete the truth tables. [8]

AND gate

A	B	Q
0	0	
0	1	
1	0	
1	1	

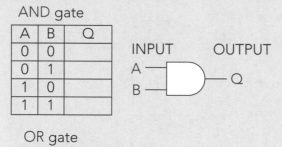

INPUT   OUTPUT

OR gate

A	B	Q
0	0	
0	1	
1	0	
1	1	

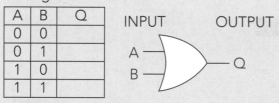

INPUT   OUTPUT

Answers can be found on page 141

Summary

You should now have an understanding of:
- how to construct truth tables for the following logic gates:
  - NOT
  - AND
  - OR

  You do not need to know about or use NAND, NOR and XOR logic gates for the AQA exam.
- how to construct truth tables for simple logic circuits

- how to interpret the results of simple truth tables
- how to construct truth tables which contain up to three inputs
- how to create, modify and interpret simple logic circuit diagrams
- how to construct simple logic circuit diagrams which contain up to three inputs.

You will be expected to understand and use logic circuit symbols.

3.4.3 Software classification 1

Types of software

There are two main types of **software**.
- Application software: These are pieces of software that perform a particular task such as word processing or desktop publishing.
- Systems software (operating systems): These types of software control the running of hardware and the running of other software.

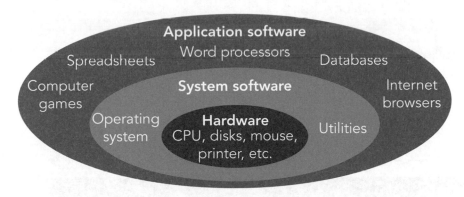

Operating systems

- An operating system is a piece of software that controls the operation of the systems hardware and the running of other software.
- Some of the most popular operating systems are:
  - Windows
  - Windows CE
  - Macintosh OS X (Mac OS X)
  - iOS (iPhoneOS)
  - Linux
  - Android Phone
  - Blackberry (RIM OS)
  - Solaris (SunOS)
  - AIX
  - IOS (Cisco)
  - XOS (Extreme Networks)
  - IronWare OS (Foundry).
- The operating system, as we can see, is actually not one but a **collection of programs** that control the system.
- The operating system is responsible for the **management and control** of all the computer's resources.
- This includes memory, processors, hard drives, **monitoring** I/O devices, etc.
- It not only handles the system resources, it also handles the application software that users run, security and file management.
- It also provides a link between the hardware and software.

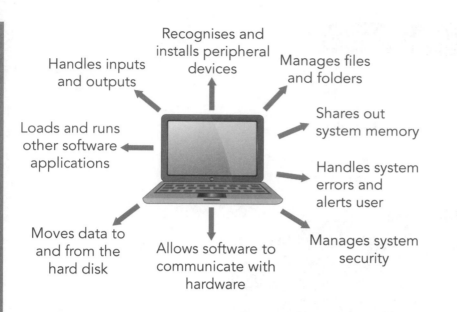

Handles inputs and outputs

Recognises and installs peripheral devices

Manages files and folders

Loads and runs other software applications

Shares out system memory

Handles system errors and alerts user

Moves data to and from the hard disk

Allows software to communicate with hardware

Manages system security

Utility software

REVISED ☐

Software	Use
Virus scanner	To protect your system from Trojans and viruses.
Disk defragmenter	To speed up your hard disk. Defragmentation picks up all those pieces of data that are spread across the drive and puts them back together again.
System monitor	To look at your current system resources.

Application software

REVISED ☐

Application software is a program that is designed to do a **particular** task. For example, word processors and games are types of application program.

Application software is computer software that causes a computer to perform useful tasks beyond the running of the computer itself.

Such software is often called a software application, program, application or app.

Examples of application software include:
● Animation software
● Audio editing
● Data manipulation (databases and spreadsheets)
● Digital audio editor
● Graphic art software
● Graphics editing
● Image editing software
● Image organisers
● Media content creating/editing
● Music sequencer
● Presentation software
● Sound editing software
● Text editors (word processors, desktop publishing)
● Vector graphics editor
● Video editing software
● Web browser.

Translation software

The purpose of translation software is to convert program source code into machine code that can be executed on the processor.

Translation software includes:

- assemblers
- compilers
- interpreters.

Each performs a different task.

Assembler	An assembler (meaning one that assembles) is a computer program which translates assembly language to an object code or machine language.
Compiler	A compiler translates the whole program (source code) into object code that can be stored and reused. A compiler makes faster, more secure code. A compiler also produces object code that is difficult to read, meaning competitors won't easily be able to steal or users hack the code.
Interpreter	Interpreters allow for code to run on multiple platforms. You can also debug and test code without having to re-compile the entire source code.

Exam practice

1 Which of the following is not a type of software? [1]
   A   system software
   B   application software
   C   utility software
   D   entertainment software

2 Programs designed to perform specific tasks are known as ... [1]
   A   system software
   B   application software
   C   utility programs
   D   operating systems

3 Operating systems, editors, and debuggers are types of ... [1]
   A   system software
   B   application software
   C   utilities
   D   none of the above

4 A computer program that converts an entire program into machine language is called a/an ... [1]
   A   interpreter
   B   simulator
   C   compiler
   D   commander

5 What do you call programs that are used to find out possible faults and their causes? [1]
   A   operating system extensions
   B   cookies
   C   diagnostic software
   D   boot diskettes

6 Which programming languages are classified as low-level languages? [1]
  A Basic, COBOL, FORTRAN
  B Prolog 2, Expert systems
  C knowledge-based systems
  D assembly languages

7 Which of the following is a machine-independent program? [1]
  A high-level language
  B low-level language
  C assembly language
  D machine language

Answers can be found on page 141

Summary

You should now have an understanding of:
● what is meant by:
  – system software
  – application software.
  You must be able to give examples of both types of software.

3.4.3 Software classification 2

Functions of operating systems

All operating systems have certain common functions:
- memory management
- file management
- security
- provision of an interface
- input/output
- error reporting
- utility software management.

Memory management

REVISED

Controls the system's **RAM**, controlling which locations in RAM programs are loaded into.

The operating system handles the computer's memory and the sharing of the central processing unit (CPU). Its job is to make sure that each application gets the correct and adequate resources.

It is also responsible for maximising the whole system.

The operating system memory management functions include:
- controlling the location of memory, dealing with the transfer of programs in and out of memory when the process no longer needs them or when the process has been ended
- carrying out a process called scheduling where it manages the CPU, organising the use of memory between programs
- organising processing time between programs and users
- keeping track of processors and the status of any process running.

File management

REVISED

Controls where and how files are saved onto backing storage.

The operating system handles the organisation and tracking of files and directories (folders). It also saves or retrieves these from a computer disk.

The operating system does the following file management activities:
- allows the user to perform tasks including the creation of files and directories
- allows the user to save files to a backing store
- allows the user to rename, copy, move and delete files
- keeps track of where files are located on the hard drive through either a file allocation table (FAT) or the New Technology File System (NTFS).

> **Exam tip**
>
> When answering MCQs try to think of the answer before you look at the choices you have been given.

Security

REVISED

Computer systems often have multiple users. These users are often running multiple processes and these processes must be secure. The operating system maintains security and access rights of users.

The operating system does the following security activities:
- controls the access of programs, processes and users to the computer resources
- ensures that all access to system resources is controlled

- ensures that external I/O devices are protected from invalid access attempts
- provides authentication features for each user by means of a password.

Provision of an interface

This is the means of interacting with the user. Most modern operating systems provide a GUI (Graphical User Interface).

Input/output

Controls the sending and receiving of data to and from peripherals.

The operating system does the following activities for device management:
- acts as the I/O comptroller by keeping track of all **I/O devices**
- decides which process gets to use the device, when and for how much time.

Error reporting

Providing useful **feedback** to users when errors do occur.

In any computer, the operating system deals with errors and user instructions. Errors can occur any time and anywhere including errors in the CPU, in I/O devices or in the memory hardware.

The operating system does the following error-management activities:
- monitors the system for any errors that occur
- takes appropriate actions to ensure correct operations
- closes the system if errors are terminal.

Exam practice

1 Discuss the role of the operating system. [8]

2 Explain the main memory management functions of the operating system. [6]

3 What is peripheral management? [6]

Answers can be found on page 141

Summary

You should now have an understanding of:
- the need for, and functions of, operating systems (OS) and utility programs
- how the OS handles management of the:
  - processor(s)
  - memory
  - I/O devices
  - applications
  - security.

3.4.4 Systems architecture 1

Von Neumann architecture

A von Neumann-based computer:

- uses one memory for both **instructions** and **data**
- cannot distinguish between data and instructions in a memory location
- **executes** programs by doing one instruction after the next in a serial manner using a fetch–decode–execute cycle.

Advantages of von Neumann architecture

- The main advantage is that it simplifies the micro-controller chip design because only one memory is accessed.
- In micro-controllers, the most important thing is the contents of RAM (random-access memory) and in the von Neumann system it can be used for both variable (data) storage and program instruction storage.
- Another advantage is that it allows greater flexibility in developing software, particularly in the development of operating systems.

Disadvantages of von Neumann architecture

- Whilst the advantages far outweigh the disadvantages, the problem is that there is only one bus (pathway) connecting the memory and the processor so only one instruction or data item can be fetched at a time. This means the processor may have to wait a long time for the data/instruction to arrive. This is referred to as the von Neumann bottleneck.
- The above problem can also lead to a system crash as there may be confusion between data and instructions.

The **hardware** within a computer system includes the CPU (central processing unit), which is situated on a printed circuit board called the motherboard.

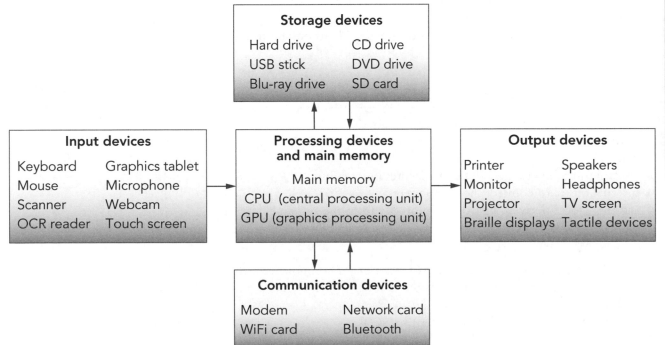

Storage devices

Hard drive	CD drive
USB stick	DVD drive
Blu-ray drive	SD card

Input devices

Keyboard	Graphics tablet
Mouse	Microphone
Scanner	Webcam
OCR reader	Touch screen

Processing devices and main memory

Main memory

CPU (central processing unit)

GPU (graphics processing unit)

Output devices

Printer	Speakers
Monitor	Headphones
Projector	TV screen
Braille displays	Tactile devices

Communication devices

| Modem | Network card |
| WiFi card | Bluetooth |

The CPU – central processing unit

- This internal device is often referred to as the 'computer's brain' and it is the piece of hardware that is responsible for the 'compute' in computer.
- If you did not have the CPU, you would not have a computer.
- The CPU's purpose is to process data and it does this by performing functions such as searching and sorting data, and calculating and decision making using the data.

What this means is that for every task you carry out on a computer, the central processing unit deals with all of the data-processing.

The CPU continuously reads instructions stored in main memory and executes them as required:
- fetch: the next instruction is fetched to the CPU from main memory
- decode: the instruction is decoded to work out what it is
- execute: the instruction is executed (carried out).

This may include reading/writing from/to main memory.

Speed

The CPU undertakes **instructions** it receives from programs in a **cycle**. The CPU not only has a number of cores; it also has speed.

Computer and microprocessor designers are driven by the need to improve computer performance to meet the ever-increasing demands of computer users.
- The speed of the CPU is measured in how many **cycles** it can perform in a second. The name given to one cycle per second is one hertz (Hz).
- Early microprocessors had **clock speeds** measured in **kHz** (thousands of cycles per second). A CPU that processes one million cycles per second is said to have a speed of one megahertz.
- A CPU that can handle one billion cycles per second is said to have a clock speed of one **gigahertz**. Obviously clock speed is an important factor in determining performance.
- Most modern processors have speeds of over 1 GHz (thousand million cycles per second).

Components of the processor

A processor contains the following components:
- **arithmetic** logic unit: performs arithmetic and **logical** operations on data
- control unit: fetches, decodes and executes instructions
- internal buses: to connect the components
- internal clock: derived directly or indirectly from the system clock.

Arithmetic and logic unit

The arithmetic logic unit (called the **ALU**) is a major component of the central processing unit of a computer system. ALUs routinely perform the following:
- logical operations: including AND, OR, NOT
- logical comparisons

Both papers

- bit-shifting operations: shifting the positions of bits by a certain number of places to the right or left, which is considered a multiplication or division operation
- arithmetic operations: bit addition and subtraction.

The control unit (CU)

The control unit (CU) is inside the CPU and is used to control the flow of data within the system. The CU:
- controls sequential instruction execution
- interprets instructions
- guides data flow through different computer areas
- regulates and controls processor timing
- sends and receives control signals from other computer devices
- handles tasks, such as fetching, decoding, execution handling and storing results.

Internal buses

- An internal bus is a type of data bus that only operates inside the computer or system. It carries data and operations like a standard bus; however, it is only used for connecting and interacting with internal computer components.
- The CPU bus is internal to the CPU and is used to transport data to and from the ALU.
- A bus is a collection of wires through which data is transmitted from one component to another. Main memory will be considered to be any form of memory that is directly accessible by the CPU, except for cache and registers.

Increasing data bus width

- Increasing the clock speed will increase the number of data fetches that can be made per second.
- Increasing the data bus width will increase the amount of data that can be fetched each time.

Internal clock

- A clock is a signal used to synchronise things inside the computer.
- The beginning of each clock cycle is when the clock signal goes from '0' to '1'.
- The clock signal is measured in a unit called hertz (Hz), which is the number of clock cycles per second. A clock signal of 100 MHz means that in one second there are 100 million clock cycles.

The clock cycle looks like this:

Factors affecting processor performance

There are a number of things in the computer architecture that can affect the processor performance. The following are the most important factors.

Number of cores

- A CPU can contain one or more processing units. Each unit is called a core.
- Each core contains an ALU, control unit and registers.

Clock speed

- The clock speed of a processor is stated in megahertz (MHz) or gigahertz (GHz).
- Basically the faster the clock, the more instructions the processor can complete per second.

On-board cache

- The on-board cache is a type of high-performance RAM built directly into the processor. Cache has both size and type.
- It enables the CPU to access repeatedly used data directly from its own on-board memory.

Cache memory

- Cache memory uses the faster but more expensive static RAM chips rather than the less expensive, but slower, dynamic RAM chips which are used for most of the main memory.
- Cache memory is connected to the processor by the 'backside' bus.
- Normally whole blocks of data are transferred from main memory into the cache, while single words are transferred along the backside bus from the cache to the processor.

L1 and L2 cache

- Most modern chips also have level 1 (L1) cache.
- This is similar to L2 cache, but the cache is actually on the same chip as the processor. This means that it is even faster to access than L2 cache.

EEPROM

EEPROM is an electrically erasable programmable read-only memory. As such, it is a user-modifiable read-only memory (ROM) and can be erased and reprogrammed without the need to be removed from the computer, as is the case with other EPROM chips. But the chip has to be erased and reprogrammed in its entirety, not selectively.

> **Exam tip**
>
> Don't spend half an hour writing a long essay for two marks – it's a waste of time as you can still only get two marks however much you write. It's better to spend the time on other parts of the question.

Exam practice

1 The central processing unit is combination of ...   [1]
    A control and storage
    B control and output unit
    C arithmetic logic and input unit
    D arithmetic logic and control unit

2 Describe cache memory and how it is used.   [6]

3 Which unit converts user data into machine-readable form? [1]
  A   input unit
  B   output unit
  C   ALU
  D   control unit

4 EEPROM stands for ... [1]
  A   electrically Erasable Programmable Read Only Memory
  B   electronic Erasable Programmable Read Only Memory
  C   easily Erasable Programmable Read Only Memory

5 Which unit is known as the nerve centre of a computer? [1]
  A   ALU
  B   CU
  C   memory
  D   registers

6 What is access time? [1]
  A   seek time + latency time
  B   seek time
  C   latency time

7 Explain the different factors affecting the processing speed of a CPU. [8]

8 Explain the general structure of a CPU. [6]

9 Which part of the computer hardware is used for calculating and comparing? [1]
  A   disk unit
  B   control unit
  C   ALU
  D   modem

10 Primary memory stores ... [1]
  A   data alone
  B   programs alone
  C   results alone
  D   all of these

Answers can be found on pages 141–2

Summary

You should now have an understanding of:
- the Von Neumann architecture
- the role and operation of main memory and the following major components of a central processing unit (CPU):
  - arithmetic logic unit
  - control unit
  - clock
  - bus
- the effect of the following on the performance of the CPU:
  - clock speed
  - number of processor cores
  - cache size
  - cache type
- the fetch–execute cycle.

3.4.4 Systems architecture 2

Storage

Secondary storage is considered to be any non-volatile storage mechanism external to the CPU.

There are two fundamentally different types of storage:
- primary store/main memory (often just called memory)
- secondary store (also known as backing store).

Main memory has the following characteristics:
- Its contents can be accessed directly by the CPU.
- It has very fast access times.
- It has a relatively small capacity.

The main/primary memory is where the operating system **resides**. This memory is divided into two types:
- Read Only Memory (ROM)
- Random Access Memory (RAM).

RAM and ROM

- The contents of RAM are lost when the computer is turned off (volatile).
- The contents of ROM are retained (non-volatile).

ROM

- ROM is memory that cannot be changed by a program or user.
- ROM retains its memory even after the computer is turned off.
- ROM is also used to store software that needs to be available when the computer is turned on (such as the instructions for **booting** the computer) or software that will 'never' change, such as the BIOS.
- With von Neumann architecture, the program(s) being run are kept in the computer memory as well as the data that is currently being processed.

RAM

- RAM is a fast temporary type of memory in which programs, applications and data are held. RAM holds things while the computer is on and running:
  - the operating system
  - applications software.
- If a computer loses power, all data stored in its RAM is lost.

Cache memory

- Cache is simply very fast memory.
- Cache memory is a special type of RAM.
- The cache is almost always located on the same microchip as the CPU.
- Traditionally cache is categorised in 'levels' that describe its closeness and the accessibility of the cache to the microprocessor.

Both papers

Cache types

- Level 1 (L1) cache is extremely fast but relatively small, and is usually **embedded** in the processor chip (CPU) which is why it is called level 1. It is closest to the processor. Level 1 cache usually ranges in size from 8 kB to 64 kB.
- Level 2 (L2) cache is often larger than L1 but one stage further from the processor. It may be located on the CPU or on a separate **chip**.
- Level 3 (L3) cache is typically specialised memory that works to improve the performance of L1 and L2. It can be significantly slower than L1 or L2, but is usually double the speed of RAM.

Accessing memory

- Memory can be accessed **sequentially** or **randomly**.

Sequential access

- To go from file A to file Z in a sequential-access system, you must pass through all files in order. Sequential access is also called serial access.

Direct/random access

- Refers to the ability to access data at random. In a **random-access** system, you can jump directly to file Z. Disks are examples of random access media.

Secondary storage

Secondary storage is used to save **permanent** copies of your files.

The majority of secondary storage devices are used for long-term storage.

They are also used to:
- backup data
- add more storage space for files/pictures/videos, etc.
- transfer files between computers
- easily transport files
- share files over a network.

There are three main types of secondary storage.
- **Magnetic:** These use **magnetic** fields to store the data.
  - Hard disk drives
  - Magnetic tapes
- **Optical:** These store data by means of lasers 'burning' a disk.
  - CD-ROM
  - DVD
  - Blue ray
- **Solid state**: This uses no moving parts at all; it uses memory chips.
  - USB drives
  - SSD hard drives

Magnetic storage devices (MSD)

A magnetic hard disk drive (HDD) uses moving read/write **heads** that contain electromagnets.

These create a magnetic charge on the disk's surface which contains iron particles that can be given a magnetic charge in one of two directions.

Each magnetic particle's direction represents 0 (off) or 1 (on). These represent a bit of data that the CPU can recognise.

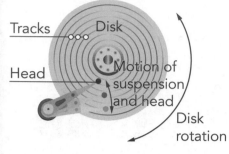

Magnetised data on disk

Tracks — Disk

Head — Motion of suspension and head

Disk rotation

Advantages of magnetic storage

- Very large data storage capacity.
- Stores and retrieves data much faster than an optical disk.
- Data is not lost when you switch off the computer as it is with RAM.
- Cheap per MB compared with other storage media.
- Can easily be replaced and upgraded.

Disadvantages of magnetic storage

- Hard disks have moving parts which can fail.
- Crashes can damage the surface of the disk, leading to loss of data.
- Easily damaged if dropped.
- Uses a large amount of power compared with other media.
- Can be noisy.

Optical storage devices (OSD)

REVISED

- An optical drive uses **reflected** light to read data.
- The optical disk's surface is covered with tiny dents (pits) and flat spots (lands), which cause light to be reflected off them differently.
- When an optical drive shines light into a pit, the light is not reflected back. This represents a bit value of 0 (off).
- When the light shines on a flat surface (land) it reflects light back to the sensor, representing a bit value of 1 (on).

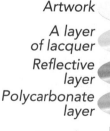

Artwork

A layer of lacquer

Reflective layer

Polycarbonate layer

Laser beam and sensor

Advantages of optical storage devices

- Easy to store and carry.
- Optical disks are read in a number of devices such as audio and TV systems.
- Very easy to use.
- Long lasting if looked after properly.

Disadvantages of optical storage devices

- Data on write-once disks (CDR, DVDR and DRR) are permanent and cannot be changed.
- Optical disks require special drives to read/write.
- Optical storage is expensive per GB/TB in comparison with other methods.
- There are no standards for longevity tests.
- Can easily be scratched and damaged by heat and light.
- Easily broken.

Solid-state disks (SSD)

Solid state disks contain no moving parts.

They are found in three common formats:
- hard disk replacements
- memory cards
- USB flash drives.

They record data using special transistors that retain their state even when there is no power to them.

Advantages of solid-state disks

- Read speeds are faster than for normal hard drives.
- Because there is no moving actuator arm like on a hard disk drive, they are faster in reading and, in some cases, writing data.
- They are also more rugged so are not as easily damaged when dropped.
- Solid-state hard drives have non-volatile memory, which means that data is stable.
- They are lightweight.
- They are very durable.
- They are free from mechanical problems.
- They require less power than magnetic drives.
- They are silent in use.

Disadvantages of solid-state disks

- They have limited storage capacity when compared with normal magnetic hard drives.
- Random write speeds of solid state drives can be four times slower than for normal magnetic hard drives.
- The cost per MB stored is higher than for magnetic drives.

Cloud storage

- Cloud storage means the storage of data online 'in the cloud'.
- In cloud storage, data is stored and is accessible from multiple distributed and connected resources that comprise a cloud via the internet.

Advantages of cloud storage

- Unlimited storage capacity. Cloud computing offers limitless storage.
- Automatic backup. On a computer, a hard disk crash can destroy all your valuable data if it is stored on the device, but if it is in the cloud a computer crash shouldn't affect any of your data.
- Universal access. You don't carry your files and documents with you, they stay in the cloud, and you access them whenever you have a computer or mobile device and an internet connection. All your documents are instantly available wherever you are.
- Device independence. The user is not limited to working on a document stored on a single computer or network. You can change computer and even change to your mobile device, and the documents follow you through the cloud.

Disadvantages of cloud storage

- Cloud storage requires a reliable internet connection. Cloud computing is impossible if you can't connect to the internet.
- Cloud storage will not work as well with low-speed connections.
- Web-based apps and large documents and images require a lot of bandwidth.
- Loss of control. The user loses control over what happens to the data as this is managed by the cloud service provider.

Given the many advantages, Apple, Google and Microsoft have all developed cloud-based storage.

Exam practice

1 Which of the following is not a primary storage device? [1]
   A magnetic tape
   B magnetic disk
   C optical disk
   D all of the above

2 What does CD-ROM stand for? [1]
   A Compactable Read Only Memory
   B Compact Data Read Only Memory
   C Compactable Disk Read Only Memory
   D Compact Disk Read Only Memory

3 Which unit converts user data into machine readable form? [1]
   A input unit
   B output unit
   C ALU
   D control unit

4 What does the disk drive of a computer do? [1]
   A rotates the disk
   B reads the disk
   C loads a program from the disk into the memory
   D reads the disk and loads a program from the disk into the memory

5 Primary memory stores ... [1]
   A data alone
   B programs alone
   C results alone
   D all of these

Answers can be found on page 142

Summary

You should now have an understanding of:
- the differences between main memory and secondary storage
- the terms 'volatile' and 'non-volatile'
- the differences between RAM and ROM
- why secondary storage is required
- the different types of secondary storage (solid state, optical and magnetic)
- SSDs using electrical circuits to persistently store data but you will not need to know the precise details such as use of NAND gates
- the operation of solid state, optical and magnetic storage
- the advantages and disadvantages of solid state, optical and magnetic storage
- the term 'cloud storage'
- cloud storage using magnetic and increasingly solid state storage at a remote location
- the advantages and disadvantages of cloud storage when compared with local storage
- the term 'embedded system' and how an embedded system differs from a non-embedded system
- examples of embedded and non-embedded systems.

Paper 2 only

3.5 Computer networks

3.5.1 Fundamentals of computer networks 1

Networks

- A computer network can be described as two or more computers connected together to share resources. The purpose of connecting computers together in a network is to exchange information and data.
- Networked computers can use resources of other computers.
- A computer network is a linked set of computer systems capable of sharing computer power and resources such as printers, large disk drives, CD-ROM and other databases.
- There are two types of network:
  - Local Area Network (LAN)
  - Wide Area Network (WAN).

> **Exam tip**
>
> If your brain freezes, just start writing anything and you will soon start remembering more details.

Local area networks (LAN)

- LANs are characterised by high-speed transmission over a restricted geographical area.
- If the LAN is too large, signals need to be boosted.
- A local area network is a computer network across one building or site. It is often owned and controlled/managed by a single person or organisation.

Wide area networks (WAN)

- While LANs operate where distances are relatively small, wide area networks (WANs) are used to link LANs that are separated by large distances that range from a few tens of metres to thousands of kilometres. WANs are often under collective or distributed ownership.
- The internet is the biggest example of a WAN.

> **Exam tip**
>
> Networks can be wired or wireless.

Advantages of computer networks

- A network allows users to share software stored in a main system.
- Files can easily be shared between users over a network.
- Network users can communicate via email, instant messenger, and VoIP.
- Within networks, it is much more straightforward to back up data as it is all stored on the file server.
- Networks allow data to be transmitted to remote areas that are connected within local areas.
- Networking computers allows users to share common peripheral resources such as printers, fax machines, etc. therefore saving money.

Disadvantages of computer networks

- The cabling to construct a network as well as the file servers can be costly.
- The management of a large network is complicated, which requires training and a specialist network manager usually needs to be employed.
- In the event of a file server breaking down, the files contained on the server become inaccessible, although email might still work if it is stored on a separate email server. The computers can still be used but are isolated.
- If a virus gets into the system through a network it can easily spread to other computers.
- There is a risk of hacking, particularly with wide area networks. Stringent security measures are required to prevent such abuse, such as a firewall.

Peer-to-peer network

- This describes a very simple network structure where shared resources such as printers are available but where there are very few other facilities.
- All computers on the network have similar specification and status.

Client–server network

- This method of network organisation requires one or more servers to which a number of clients may obtain services.
- The servers act as central resource managers for the network.
- A star topology is often used for this form of network.

Network hardware

REVISED

Network hardware includes:
- workstations
- servers
- passive components such as cables, connections, etc.
- active components such as repeaters, hubs, switches.

Network interface card (NIC)

- Used to connect a computer to a network.

There are two different types:
- wired
- wireless.

Transmission medium

- Transmission medium is the material used to carry data over the network.

There are two main forms:
- wired – using cables
- wireless – WiFi.

Wired

Two types of cables are most commonly used:
- unshielded twisted pair (UTP) – copper wire
  - Prone to interference – data carried using electrical signals.
  - Can be tapped.
  - Fairly cheap to install.

- optical fibre – fine strands of glass – data carried using beams of light.
  - ○ Although more expensive does not corrode.
  - ○ Secure data transmission.
  - ○ Much higher bandwidth over a much longer distance.

Coaxial	Twisted pair	Fibre optic
Electrical signal communication via the wires	Electrical signal communication via inner conductor of the wires	Optical signal communication via the glass fibres
High noise contamination	Medium noise contamination	Very low noise contamination
Can be affected by external magnetic interference	Less affected by external magnetic interference	Not affected by magnetic interference
Low bandwidth	Medium bandwidth	High bandwidth
Lowest cost of the three communication media	Moderately expensive compared with coaxial cable	Most expensive of the three communication media

Wireless

Router

Possible methods of data transmission are:

Bluetooth
- Temporary short-range links between devices such as mobile phones, headsets, laptops.
- Has a maximum range of 10 metres.
- Transfer rate of between 1 and 3 Mbps.

WiFi
- Used in laptop computers, wireless routers, mobile phones and game consoles.
- Home WiFi should be protected with a hard-to-guess password to prevent other people from using your broadband.
- If your broadband is stolen the thief may be liable for prosecution, however, if they use it to do something illegal, you may be held responsible.

Advantages and benefits of wireless networks

- The primary benefit of a wireless network is the freedom from cables.
- It is also very convenient. The wireless nature of WiFi networks allows users to access network resources from almost any convenient location.
- With the growth of public wireless networks, users can also access the internet outside their normal work or home environment.
- The initial setup of an infrastructure-based wireless network is relatively low cost as it requires no expensive cabling and a small network needs just a single access point.
- Wireless networks are also easily expanded.

Risks and disadvantages of wireless networks

- Any time data is sent wirelessly, there is a chance that it can be intercepted.
- The security used to encrypt the information determines how easy or hard it is to intercept the data.
- A WiFi range, whilst sufficient for a typical home, can be insufficient in a larger building.
- The speed on most wireless networks is much slower than on the slowest common wired networks. In some situations where speed is essential, a user may need a wired network.

Bandwidth

Bandwidth is the amount of data that can be carried over a network at any one time.

Data transfer speed means the same as bandwidth.

It is measured in:
- Mbps – megabits per second
- Gbps – gigabits per second.

Any electronic communications process requires the following components:
- a source of information
- a transmitter to convert the information into data signals compatible with the communications channel
- a communications channel
- a receiver to convert the data signals back into a form the destination can understand
- the destination of the information.

The transmitter encodes the information into a suitable form to be transmitted over the communications channel.

The communications channel moves this signal as electromagnetic energy from the source to one or more destination receivers.

The channel may convert this energy from one form to another. This could be electrical or optical signals. It must maintain the integrity of the information so the recipient can understand the message sent by the transmitter.

Network stations

The network station (often called the client) will normally comprise:
- a PC
- a network interface card (NIC). The NIC allows the computer to communicate with the network.
- network operating systems.

Servers

- A network server is a computer which acts as a central storage point for files and applications.
- Servers also act as a connection point to shared peripherals such as printers.
- Active components are required for all but the simplest of networks.
- These include:
  - repeaters
  - hubs
  - switches.

Repeaters

- Due to loss of **signal** strength it is often necessary to use a repeater to boost the signal.
- A repeater is a hardware device to link together two cable segments.
- The repeater amplifies the signal it receives before passing it on.

Hubs

- A hub is a device which allows the **interconnection** of a group of users.
- A hub will forward any packet of data it receives over one port from one station to all of the remaining ports.
- Hubs are used in the star topology.

Switches

- A switch is 'smarter' than a hub and offers more bandwidth.
- A switch forwards data packets only to the appropriate port for the intended recipient.
- The switch establishes a temporary connection between the source and the destination.

Routers

- A router receives packets of data transmitted over a network and, using their IP address, forwards them to the correct destinations over the most efficient available path.

Network topology

- The network topology is the theoretical arrangement of components on a network.
- There are two network **topologies** which you need to be aware of:
  - bus
  - star.

Paper 2 only

Bus topology

- Each device is connected to a main communications line called a **bus**.
- A single cable that functions as the backbone of the network acts as a shared communication medium that devices connect to via an interface connector.
- When a device wishes to communicate with another network device, it transmits a broadcast message onto the 'backbone' wire.

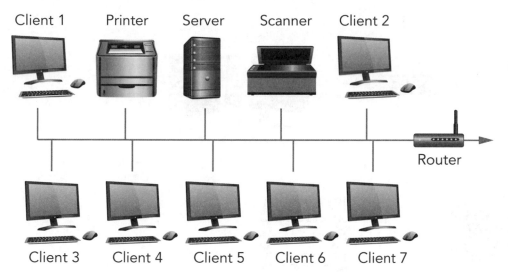

Advantages of bus topology

- It is easy and cheaper than other types of wired network to install as a consequence of requiring only a small quantity of cable.
- The lack of **dependency** on a central device which is present in a star topology makes the system more flexible.

Disadvantages of bus topology

- It performs well only for a limited number of computers because as more devices are connected the performance of the network becomes slower as a **consequence** of data collisions.
- The impact of a single cable failure makes this type of wired network more vulnerable than other wired networks.

Star topology

- In the star topology all stations are connected to a central **node**, called a hub.
- Nearly all wired home networks use the star topology.
- This topology is, therefore, better understood than many other networks.
- The star network has a central connection point referred to as a '**hub** node' that could be a device such as network hub, **switch** or router.
- The router on its own cannot be the hub node of a network. It needs to be linked to a switch although in practice, they are usually in the same box.

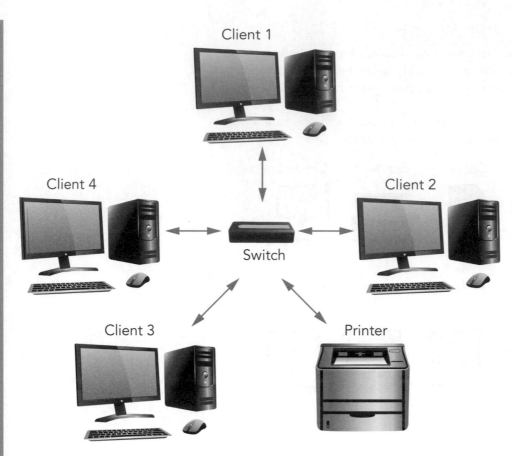

Advantages of star topology

- Compared with bus topology, star topology is better in terms of **performance** as signals don't necessarily get transmitted to all the workstations, although performance does depend on the capacity of the central hub.
- The transmission medium is not shared so there can be multiple simultaneous communications.
- Failure of one node or link doesn't affect the rest of network and it is easy to detect a failure and troubleshoot it as it allows isolation of each device within the network.

Disadvantages of star topology

- The network operation ultimately relies on the correct **functioning** of the central hub. So if the central hub crashes it will lead to the failure of the whole network.
- The use of a hub, router or switch as the central device and the additional cabling costs increase the overall cost of the network.
- Performance and the number of nodes which can be added depend on the capacity of the central device.

Exam practice

1 What is a computer network? [2]

2 What is a file server? [2]

3 What is a workstation? [1]

4 WAN stands for … [1]
   A Wap Area Network
   B Wide Area Network
   C Wide Array Net
   D Wireless Area Network

5 What are routers? [2]

6 What are switches? [2]

7 State TWO different data transmission methods. [2]

8 What is a network topology? [2]

9 List FIVE advantages and FIVE disadvantages of using computer networks. [10]

Answers can be found on pages 142–3

Summary

You should now have an understanding of:
- what a computer network is
- the benefits and risks of computer networks
- the main types of computer network including:
  - Personal Area Network (PAN)
  - Local Area Network (LAN)
  - Wide Area Network (WAN)
  - PAN – Bluetooth needs to be considered
- how wired networks can use different types of cable such as fibre and copper and when each would be appropriate

- the benefits and risks of wireless networks as opposed to wired networks
- the bus and star network topologies
- how to draw topology diagrams and the differences between the two topologies
- how to select the most appropriate topology for a given scenario.

3.5.1 Fundamentals of computer networks 2

Protocols

- A protocol is a standard set of **rules** used to ensure the proper transfer of data between devices.
- In network design it is vital that a recognised protocol is used.
- You should be aware that the network layer is sometimes referred to as the internet layer and that the data link layer is sometimes referred to as the network **interface** layer.

IP addressing

- Every computer station on the network must have an IP address.
- This IP address must be unique but is not encoded in the network interface. It is set by software in the computer.
- Internet addressing is similar to the postal addressing system.
- The address system on the internet is called Internet Protocol (IP) addressing. In IPv4 an IP address assigned to a host is 32 bits long and is unique.
- An IP address has two parts:
  - one part that is similar to the postal code
  - the other part that is similar to the house address.
- They are known as the net id (netid) and the host id (hostid).
- The netid identifies a contiguous block of addresses and is used to identify which particular network the host is located on.

Mac address

- Another popular form of address is the Media Access Control (MAC) address.
- MAC addresses are six bytes (48 bits) long.
- The computer's own hardware configuration determines its MAC address.
- The configuration of the network it is connected to determines its IP address.
- The first half of a MAC address contains the ID number of the adapter manufacturer.
- The second half of a MAC address represents the serial number assigned to the adapter by the manufacturer.

TCP/IP

- All networked computers communicate through protocol **suites**.
- The most widely used and most widely available protocol suite is the TCP/IP protocol suite.
- TCP/IP is a protocol which allows computers on different networks to communicate.
- TCP/IP is a pair of protocols:
  - TCP – transmission control protocol
  - IP – internet protocol.

Paper 2 only

- TCP/IP is a four-layer system.
  - Application layer: this is where the network applications, such as web browsers or email programs, operate.
  - Transport layer: this layer sets up the communication between the two hosts and they agree settings such as 'language' and **size of packets**.
  - Network layer: addresses and packages data for transmission. Routes the packets across the network.
  - Data link layer: this is where the network hardware such as the **NIC** (network interface card) is located. OS device drivers also sit here.

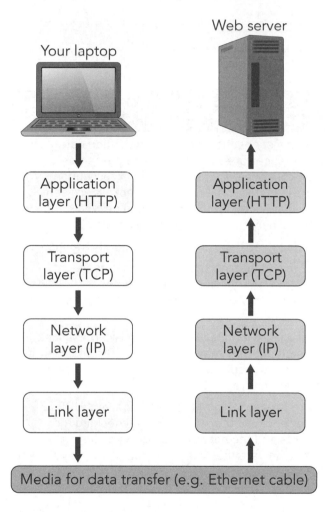

The application layer

The application layer provides applications for file **transfer**, remote control, and internet activities.

Some of the most common application layer protocols are:
- FTP (File Transfer Protocol): a standard network protocol that is used to transfer computer files from one host to another host.
- HTTP (Hypertext Transfer Protocol): HTTP is the underlying protocol used by the World Wide Web.
- IMAP (Internet Message Access Protocol): IMAP is an internet standard protocol used by email clients to retrieve email messages from a mail server.
- HTTPS (HTTP Secure): a protocol for secure communication over a computer network.

- SMTP (Simple Mail Transfer Protocol): a TCP/IP protocol used in sending and receiving email. As it is limited in its ability to queue messages at the receiving end, it is usually used with one of two other protocols, POP3 or IMAP.
- SNMP (Simple Network Management Protocol): created as a way of gathering information from different networked systems in a consistent way.

The transport layer

REVISED

Below the application layer is the transport layer. It is the main interface for all network applications.

The most commonly used transport layer protocols are:
- TCP
- UDP.

Differences between TCP and UDP	
TCP	**UDP**
Data is read as a byte stream. No distinguishing indications are transmitted to signal the message (segment) boundaries. TCP is a connection-oriented protocol. If a connection is lost, the server requests the lost part.	UDP is a connectionless protocol. When data or messages are sent, there is no guarantee they will arrive. There may also be corruption while transferring a message. Packets are sent individually and are guaranteed to be whole if they arrive. There is one packet per one read call.
TCP is more complex but reliable.	UDP is faster but provides no reliability mechanism.
TCP is suited for applications that require high reliability, and transmission time is relatively less critical.	UDP is suitable for applications that need fast, efficient transmission, such as games. UDP is also useful for servers that answer small queries from huge numbers of clients.
If two messages are sent along a connection, one after the other, the first message arrives first. Data cannot arrive in the wrong order.	Messages are not ordered. When two messages are sent out they may arrive in a different order. If ordering is required, it has to be managed by the application layer.
Data is read as a 'stream', with nothing distinguishing where one packet ends and the next begins. There may be multiple packets per read call.	There is no tracking of connections, etc. UDP is faster because there is no error-checking for packets and the network card/OS has less work to do to translate the data back from the sent packets.

The network layer

REVISED

- The network layer provides an interface with the physical network.
- The network layer is responsible for routing, which is moving packets across the network using the most appropriate paths.
- It also addresses messages and translates logical addresses (i.e. IP addresses) into physical addresses (i.e. MAC addresses). The main purpose of this layer is to organise or handle the movement of data on the network.
- The main protocol used at this **layer** is IP.
- This layer also **formats** the data for transmission and provides error control for data delivered on the physical network.

The data link layer

- The data link layer is sometimes known as the network **interface** layer.
- The data link layer is where most LAN (local area network) and wireless LAN technologies are defined.
- This layer normally consists of device drivers in the OS and the network interface card attached to the system.
- The data link layer is the protocol layer in a program that handles the moving of data in and out across a **physical** link in a network.
- The device drivers and the network interface card control all communications with the media being used and transfer the data over the network.

The most commonly used data link layer protocols are:
- ARP (Address Resolution Protocol)
- PPP (Point to Point Protocol).

The data link layer is **responsible** for encoding bits into packets prior to transmission and then decoding the packets back into bits at the destination.

The data link layer is also responsible for logical link control, media access control, hardware addressing, error detection and handling, and defining physical layer standards.

The data link layer processes data faster than the network layer because less analysis of the packet is required.

Data packets

- Anything sent between computers has to be divided up into **packets**.
- Packets are small data units.
- Transmitted packets have to be put back together in the correct order.
- These protocols wrap each data packet with a set of instructions.
- The name for this is **encapsulation**.
- Once all the packets have been received, the client needs to know they have all arrived so the very last packet is a special one called a **frame**.

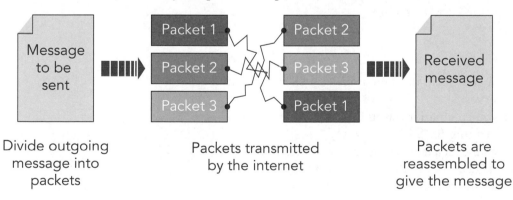

Divide outgoing message into packets

Packets transmitted by the internet

Packets are reassembled to give the message

Email protocols

When you send and receive an email there are three different protocols that can be used to **handle** the email:

● IMAP
● POP
● SMTP.

IMAP and POP are used to receive mail. SMTP is used to send mail.

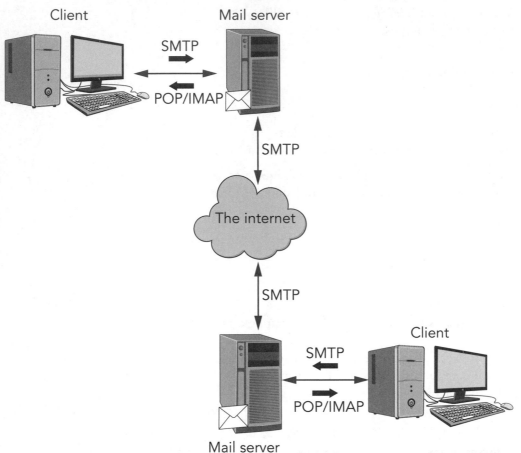

Receiving emails

● The software you use on your local machine is called a client and this is connected to a mail server.
● When someone sends you an email it travels from the sender's email client to their mail server using SMTP.
● Their mail server then uses the recipient's email address to determine where the mail should be sent and delivers it to the receiver's mail server.
● The receiver's mail server stores the received email in a mailbox until the receiver's mail client asks for it.
● IMAP and POP are the two main protocols used for retrieving email from a **mail server**.
● Both protocols are supported by almost all popular mail client programs including Outlook and Apple Mail.
● The IMAP protocol, by default, allows the user to keep all messages on the server.
● It constantly synchronises the email client program with the server and displays what messages are currently there. All the actions performed on the messages are carried out directly on the server.

- The POP protocol is set by **default** to **download** all the messages from the email server onto the client device.
- This means that all the actions performed on the messages (reading, moving, deleting …) are performed on the client machine.
- Because everything is kept on the **client** machine, the user cannot reopen messages from any machine other than where the messages have been downloaded.
- There is an option to set up the POP protocol to save a copy of the message on the server after downloading it on the client device.

Sending emails

- When you send an email you will always use some form of SMTP, which is a totally different **protocol** to IMAP and POP.
- When you click on Send for an email message, your mail client contacts the SMTP server.
- The server authenticates who the user is using the login id and password, then receives the email message from your client.
- The mail client then places the sent email in either the **local** sent mail folder or, in the case of IMAP, the sent email folder on the server.

Exam practice

1 Briefly describe the purpose of the Internet Message Access Protocol. [2]

2 Briefly describe the purpose of Post Office Protocol. [2]

3 Briefly describe the purpose of SMTP. [2]

4 Briefly describe the purpose of the Internet Protocol. [2]

Answers can be found on page 143

Summary

You should now have an understanding of:
- what each protocol is used for (e.g. HTTPS provides an encrypted version of HTTP for more secure web transactions)
- how Ethernet is a family of related protocols rather than a single protocol You do not need to know the individual protocols that make up the Ethernet family
- how WiFi is a family of related protocols rather than a single protocol
- the four-layer TCP/IP model:
  - application layer
  - transport layer
  - network layer
  - data link layer
- the layers and their main function(s) in a networking environment
- how the HTTP, HTTPS, SMTP, IMAP and FTP protocols operate at the application layer
- how the TCP and UDP protocols operate at the transport layer
- how the IP protocol operates at the network layer.

3.6 Fundamentals of cyber security

3.6.1 Cyber security threats 1

- Penetration testing is the process of attempting to gain access to resources without knowledge of usernames, passwords and other normal means of access.
- The aim of a **white-box** penetration test is to simulate a malicious insider who has knowledge of and possibly basic credentials for the target system.
- The aim of a **black-box** penetration test is to simulate an external hacking or cyber warfare attack.

Social engineering

REVISED

Social engineering is a non-technical method used by hackers to gain access to data and to systems. It relies heavily on human interaction and often involves tricking people into breaking normal security procedures.

- Virus writers use social engineering to persuade people to run malware-laden email attachments.
- Phishers use social engineering to convince people to give them **sensitive** personal information.
- Scareware hackers use social engineering to frighten people into running software that is useless at best and dangerous at worst.

Blagging

Blagging is the act of creating and using an invented **scenario** to engage a targeted victim in a manner that increases the chance that the victim will divulge information or perform actions that would be unlikely in ordinary circumstances.

Phishing

Phishing is used to attempt to **persuade** someone to enter confidential data, for example, usernames, passwords and credit card details, by **pretending** to be from a trustworthy source. It is usually carried out by email spoofing or instant messaging. Users are often asked to enter details at a fake website which looks just like the proper version.

Pharming

Pharming is a **scamming** practice in which malicious code is installed on a personal computer or server or DNS records are modified, misdirecting users to **fraudulent** websites without their knowledge or **consent**.

Shouldering (or shoulder surfing)

Shouldering, also sometimes called 'shoulder surfing', is using direct **observation** techniques, such as looking over someone's **shoulder**, to get passwords, PINs, security codes, and similar personal data.

Exam practice

1 Briefly describe the term 'phishing'. [2]

2 Briefly describe the term 'shoulder surfing' [2]

3 Briefly describe the term 'pharming'. [3]

4 Briefly describe the term 'spam'. [2]

5 Describe the term 'spoofing'. [3]

6 State what is meant by the term 'impersonation'. [2]

Answers can be found on page 143

Summary

You should now have an understanding of:
- the term 'cyber security' and the main purposes of cyber security
- how cyber security consists of the processes, practices and technologies designed to protect networks, computers, programs and data from attack, damage or unauthorised access
- the following cyber security threats:
  – social engineering techniques
  – malicious code
  – weak and default passwords
  – misconfigured access rights
  – removable media
  – unpatched and/or outdated software
- what penetration testing is and what it is used for
- what social engineering is and how it can be protected against
- the following forms of social engineering:
  – blagging (pretexting)
  – phishing
  – charming
  – shouldering (or shoulder surfing).

3.6.1 Cyber security threats 2

Malicious code: Malware

Malware is an umbrella term used to refer to a variety of forms of hostile or intrusive software.

- Viruses, keyloggers, worms and many other software attacks are different types of malicious code.
- They are often confused and thought of as being the same thing.
- They are pieces of code that are able to replicate themselves.
- However, they are distinctly different with respect to the techniques they use and their host system requirements. This distinction is due to the way they attack the host systems.

Adware

Also known as advertising-supported software. This is any software package that automatically shows adverts, such as a pop-up. They may also be in the user interface of a software package or on an installation screen. The main object of adware is to generate revenue for its author. Adware, by itself, is harmless. However, some adware may include spyware such as keyloggers.

Computer virus

A computer virus is a self-replicating program that attaches itself to existing programs and can then easily spread from one computer to another.

Viruses can increase their chances of spreading to other computers by linking to files on a network system. A virus attempts to make a computer system or data files unreliable.

Denial of service (DoS) attacks

This is an attempt to make a computer or network system unavailable to its users. A DoS attack is usually focused on preventing an internet site or service from functioning efficiently, or at all, temporarily or indefinitely. The attacks usually target sites or services hosted on high-profile web servers such as banks and payment websites (for example, PayPal).

Hacking

Hacking means finding out weaknesses in an established system and exploiting them. A computer hacker is a person who finds out weaknesses in a computer system to gain unauthorised access. A hacker may be motivated by a multitude of reasons, such as profit, protest or challenge.

Keyloggers

A keylogger is a type of spyware that logs the keys used and can collect data from an infected computer, including personal information such as websites visited, user logins and financial information.

Other malware

- A **Trojan** horse is non-replicating, malicious code contained inside of what appears to be a useful program.
- A **worm** is a self-replicating program that does not alter files, but resides in active memory and propagates itself by means of computer networks to consume resources.
- **Spyware** is a non-replicating program used to track user activities, monitor their machines and relay personal information to attackers.
- A **file infector** virus is malware that copies itself into other program files (exe, dll, bin, sys, com, drv). When the infected file is executed it loads into memory and tries to infect other files. It is also known as a parasitic virus.
- A **polymorphic** virus is malware that changes its form each time it is executed, avoiding detection/removal by antivirus software.
- A **virus hoax** is an email message that warns users of a non-existent virus or other malware.

Measures for protecting your personal data from cyber attacks

REVISED

- Do not give out personal information over the phone, on the web or in an email unless completely sure of the **recipient**. Always verify the authenticity of requests for any personal information.
- Encrypt your data.
- Keep your operating system, browser, anti-virus and other critical software up to date.
- Never click on links in emails. Even if you do think the email is legitimate, go to the website and log on directly. Be **suspicious** of any unknown links or requests sent through email or text messages.
- Never open an email attachment unless you know it is from a reliable source and turn off the option to automatically **download** attachments in emails.
- Set secure passwords and don't share them with anyone.
- Avoid using **common** words, phrases or personal information in your passwords.

Measures for protecting a network and computers from cyber attacks

REVISED

- **Encrypt** the data.
- Ensure that any HTTP open sessions **time out** after a reasonable time.
- Ensure that TCP connections time out after a reasonable time.
- Install a firewall.
- Install anti-**malware** and anti-virus protection.
- Lock the network. Many cyber attack victims are compromised via WiFi networks.
- The best defence is to have no wireless network at all. Wired networks, while less versatile due to the need for cables, are more secure. If you use WiFi, update it regularly to the latest encryption standard.
- Secure the hardware. **Physically** locking computers to a desk using the small metal loop found on most laptop and desktop devices prevents theft and access to network login data.
- Use **tracking** software on all networked mobile devices.

Exam practice

1 Briefly describe the two main functions of a computer virus.   [4]

2 Explain with examples the term 'computer virus'.   [6]

3 Describe the term 'Trojan horse'.   [2]

4 State how worms differ from viruses.   [2]

5 State what the term 'spyware' refers to.   [2]

6 State what the term 'adware' refers to.   [2]

7 Describe the term 'insider attack'.   [2]

Answers can be found on page 143

Summary

You should now have an understanding of:
● the term 'malware'
● what malware is and how it can be protected against
● these forms of malware:
  – computer virus
  – Trojan
  – spyware
  – adware.

3.6.2 Methods to detect and prevent cyber security threats

Firewalls

Basic problem
- Many network applications and protocols have security problems that are fixed over time.
- Difficult for users to keep up with changes and keep the host secure.

Solution
- Administrators limit access to end hosts by using a firewall.
- Firewalls are kept up to date by administrators.
- A firewall is a network security system that monitors and controls all incoming and outgoing network data transfer based on a set of security rules.

Firewalls can be either hardware or software.

Hardware firewalls can be purchased as stand-alone hardware but they are also often found in broadband routers.

Software firewalls are software based and must be installed on the computer. The software can then be customised.

Firewalls use a number of techniques to prevent harmful information from getting through the security wall and these include:
- packet filtering: looking at the data in each packet entering or leaving the network
- application gateway filtering: applying security mechanisms or blocking services such as FTP
- proxy server filtering: intercepting all messages entering and leaving the network and hiding the true network address.

In addition to limiting access to computers and the networks they are connected to, firewalls can be used to allow remote access to a private network using secure authentication.

> **Exam tip**
>
> AQA exam questions will be taken from the following areas:
> - cyber security
> - mobile technologies
> - wireless networking
> - cloud storage
> - theft of computer code
> - issues around copyright of algorithms
> - cracking
> - hacking
> - wearable technologies
> - computer-based implants.

Encryption

- Encryption is required when someone enters personal information or banking information on the internet to make a purchase.
- But the same encryption that can be of benefit can be of use to a terrorist.
- Even the information that you enter through an encrypted connection could be accessible online by a criminal.

Intrusion detection

- Used to monitor for '**suspicious** activity' on a network.
- Can protect against known software exploits, like buffer overflows.

HTTPS

- Hypertext transfer protocol secure (HTTPS) is a **secure** version of HTTP.
- It is HTTP that is used for the data that is sent between your browser and the website that you are connected to. The 'S' at the end of HTTPS stands for secure.
- It means all communications between your browser and the website will be encrypted.
- HTTPS uses one of two secure protocols to **encrypt** the data communications: SSL (secure sockets layer) or TLS (transport layer security).
- Both the TLS and SSL protocols use an 'asymmetric' public key infrastructure (PKI) system.
- When your browser requests a HTTPS connection, the website will first send its SSL certificate to your browser. This certificate contains the public key needed to begin a secure data session.
- Based on this initial exchange, your browser and the website then initiate the 'SSL **handshake**'.

MAC address filtering

- Media access control (MAC) addresses identify every device on your network.
- A MAC address is an **alphanumeric** string separated by colons, like this: 00:03:D1:1A:2D:14.
- Networked devices use this address as identification when they send and receive data over the network.
- In MAC address filtering, you find the MAC address of every device you want to allow on your network, and then you fill out a table in the router's user interface so that any device on the list can join your network.

Automatic updates and patches

- If your device seems to be working fine, you may wonder why you should apply a **patch** or software update.
- By not applying a patch you might be leaving the door open for malware to come in.
- Malware **exploits** flaws in a system in order to do its work, and updates and patches are designed to close these doors as they are found.

Passwords

- Passwords are **inconvenient** but necessary to protect your personal data.
- If you use the same password on all your devices and accounts, your data and your devices will also be vulnerable to **malware** and **hackers**.

When you create a password, don't use:
- dictionary words or names in any form
- common misspellings of dictionary words
- the name of the computer or your account
- sample passwords.

When you create a password, use:
- multiple character sets
- capital and lower case letters
- letters changed to numbers, for example 0 for o and 5 for s
- letters chosen from words in a phrase or song lyric
- combinations of a few pronounceable 'nonsense' words with punctuation.

Biometrics

REVISED

Biometrics are authentication techniques that rely upon the user's measurable physical characteristics that can be automatically checked. They can included:
- fingerprints
- facial recognition
- hand geometry
- iris recognition
- signature
- voice patterns.

Security misconfiguration vulnerabilities

REVISED

- When any of the **components** that make up a web application are configured badly there is a target for attackers.
- Security misconfiguration **vulnerabilities** can happen at platform level, web server level, application server level and through custom code.
- In order to provide a secure system, all the component parts of a network application need to be configured correctly.

There are many ways that **misconfiguration** can lead to security vulnerabilities.

To protect from these vulnerabilities, a number of steps need to be taken:
- Keep software up to date by installing the latest updates and security patches.
- Remove unused features including the removal all the sample applications that come with content delivery systems.
- Disable default accounts and change passwords. You should also change usernames, passwords and ports for default accounts.
- Develop a strong application architecture that effectively isolates components and encrypts data. Ensure security settings are set to secure values.
- Run tools, such as automated scanners, to check for vulnerabilities.
- Secure all layers individually and don't rely on one layer in a web application providing security for layers lower down in the stack.

Unpatched and/or outdated software vulnerabilities

REVISED

- Software vulnerabilities, like malware, have serious **security** implications.
- The **companies** that sell software are aware of these security vulnerabilities and regularly release security updates to address these flaws.
- **Outdated** and **unpatched** devices present a major security risk as the unpatched software remains weak, leaving the user open to **cyber-crime** attacks.

- Updating systems with the latest security patches protects against attacks that exploit vulnerabilities.
- Applying security updates often also addresses technical issues with the software and improves the software's **performance**.

CAPTCHA

- CAPTCHA stands for '**Completely Automated Public Turing test** to tell Computers and Humans Apart'.
- It is a program used by some websites to provide further protection for a user's password by verifying that user input is not computer-generated.
- There are now a wide number of different CAPTCHA systems using images, numbers and even simple calculations, but basically the idea is to create something that humans can read but current computer programs can't.

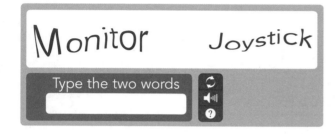

Email verification

- Email **confirmation** and CAPTCHA are used to solve different problems.
- Email verification is used to check that users are using their real email address in the registration process.
- Email **verification** is where an email is sent to the user's email address and they have to click on a link in it to confirm that the email address is theirs.
- Email **confirmation** also protects from identity theft.
- For example, the user cannot register a government email address.

Mobile phone verification

- With mobile phone **verification**, you ask the user to enter their mobile phone number.
- Then you send them an SMS (text message) with a code and they must enter this code into a web form on the website.

Exam practice

1 List FOUR possible threats to a computer system and FOUR possible security measures. [4]

2 Briefly describe why a user should apply patches and updates to their software. [6]

3 A school decides to block communication with websites that do not use HTTPS. Discuss the term HTTPS. [6]

Answers can be found on pages 143–4

Summary

You should now have an understanding of:

- these security measures:
  - biometric measures (particularly for mobile devices)
  - password systems
  - CAPTCHA (or similar)
  - using email confirmations to confirm a user's identity
  - automatic software updates
- the need for, and importance of, network security
- these methods of network security:
  - authentication
  - encryption
  - firewall
  - MAC address filtering
- what each of these security methods is and when each could be used
- how these methods can work together to provide a greater level of security
- how MAC address filtering allows devices to access, or be blocked from accessing, a network based on their physical address embedded within the device's network adapter.

3.7 Ethical, legal and environmental impacts of digital technology on wider society, including issues of privacy

Ethical use

If you access, view or collect **confidential** material and/or personal information, it is your responsibility to maintain confidentiality.

Do not share this information with **unauthorised** individuals.

Ethics and the law are not the same thing.
- **Ethics** relates to the rules and standards governing the conduct of an individual with others.
- As technology and computers became more and more a part of our everyday lives a new definition of ethics evolved, called computer ethics.
- Computer ethics is concerned with standards of **conduct** as they relate to computers.

Ethics	The law
Ethics are a guideline for computer users and are not legally enforceable.	The law consists of rules to control computer users that are legally enforceable.
Computer users are free to follow or ignore a code of ethics.	Computer users must follow the regulations and law for the country they live in.
Ethical rules are universal and can be applied anywhere, all over the world.	Laws depend on the country and state where the crime is committed. There are many examples of laws in one country allowing things that are illegal in others. This is a big issue with the internet.
Ethics aims to create ethical computer users.	Laws aim to prevent misuse of computers.
If you don't follow ethical rules you are deemed to be immoral.	Not obeying laws is referred to as crime.

Computer ethics are moral guidelines that govern the use of computers and information systems.

The digital divide

- Over the past few years, society's **dependence** on computer technology has increased.
- The ability to communicate via email and access the internet has become an essential part of everyday life.
- But there are many people in the world who do not have access to the internet and this has led to a disparity called the **digital divide**. This gap is of growing concern.
- Rural communities, low-income families, people with disabilities and areas of the wider world do not have the same advantages as more privileged households and communities.
- To many people this is a major **ethical** issue.

> **Exam tip**
>
> Read through all the questions, quickly answering all the ones you definitely know first and leaving the harder ones until last.

Intellectual property

There are laws relating to copyright and intellectual property.

- Intellectual property is about creations of the **intellect** (hence the name): inventions, artistic works, names, images and designs.
- Intellectual property also relates to industrial property, such as inventions, trademarks, etc.
- The word **property** means a possession, something in which the owner has legal rights.
- Unlike **intellectual property**, copyright law only protects the form of expressions of ideas, not the ideas themselves. So copyright laws do not protect ideas or systems, only how they are expressed.
- This means that nothing in copyright laws prevents others from developing another work based on the same idea.

Software theft

Software theft occurs when someone:

- steals software media
- illegally copies a program
- illegally registers and/or activates a program.

> **Exam tip**
>
> Remember to leave yourself some time at the end to go back over your answers and add in little notes or pieces of information about the topic. You never know, this could help bump you up a grade!

Environmental impacts of technology

- When you use computer electronics, you are participating in one **phase** of that product's life.
- Before the product makes it to you, raw materials (resources) are taken (extracted) from the environment.
- These are then processed and manufactured into a product.
- The product is packaged and transported, again using valuable resources.
- The next stage is the use of the product and the **energy** needed for this use.
- The final stage is how you **dispose** of the device when you replace it.

What can individuals do?

- Everyone has a **responsibility** to reduce their individual carbon footprint.
- Completely powering off computing devices when not in use is good for your devices and for the planet.

Other things that could be done include:

- changing power settings so that devices power down after 15 minutes of inactivity
- considering end-of-life management for all computing devices
- dimming the screens on computing devices as this saves power
- disabling screensavers as they don't actually conserve energy, some even use more energy than normal use
- not having too many programs running at the same time and change the system settings to reduce programs that auto-start
- shutting down all devices at the end of the working day
- turning off printers, scanners and other peripherals when not using them
- unplugging all computing devices when they are fully charged, otherwise they will be using power to keep topping themselves up throughout the day
- unplugging chargers when they're not in use to save on power consumption
- using hibernate instead of sleep mode.

Exam practice

1 Discuss the recent changes in shopping and shopping habits due to computing advancements. [6]

2 Discuss the issues around personal web security. [8]

Answers can be found on page 144

Summary

You should now have an understanding of:
- the current ethical, legal and environmental influences and risks of digital technology on society
- how ordinary citizens normally value their privacy and may not like it when governments or security services have too much access
- how governments and security services often argue that they cannot keep their citizens safe from terrorism and other attacks unless they have access to private data.

Exam practice answers

3.1.1 Representing algorithms

1 USERINPUT ← length
  USERINPUT ← width
  area ← length * width
  OUTPUT area

2 The basic building blocks are: sequential, selection and looping.
   • Sequential: Set, Input, and Output statements
   • Selection: Conditional, If and If-else statements
   • Looping: Iteration, While loops

3

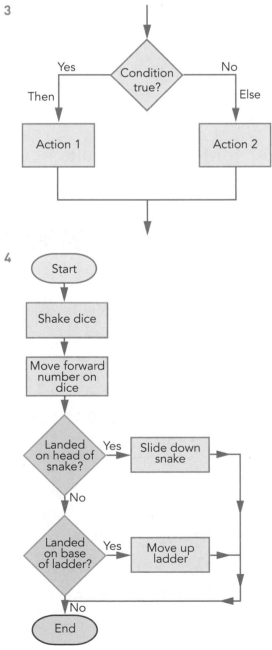

4

5 C High level

3.1.2 Efficiency of algorithms

1 It is a measure of the amount of time for an algorithm to execute.

2 • It must work.
   • It must complete its task in a finite (reasonable) amount of time.

3 C Time and space

4 B Counting the number of key operations

3.1.3 Searching algorithms

1 It is simple and useful when the elements to be searched are not in any definite order.

2 D The item is the last element in the array or is not there at all

3 A The item is somewhere in the middle of the array

4 • Linear search
   • Binary search

5 This search method starts at the beginning of the list and compares each element in turn with the required value until a match is found or the end of the list is reached.

6 D None of the above

7 C Arrays

8 B Searching

3.1.4 Sorting algorithms

1 D Traversal

2 A bubble sort is a sort in which the first two items to be sorted are examined and exchanged if necessary to place them in the required order. The second item is then compared with the third (exchanging them if required); the third is compared with the fourth, etc.

  The process is repeated until all pairs have been examined and all items are in the proper sorted order.

3 A merge sort cuts the array in half, sorting the left half and the right half independently, then merging together the two sorted halves.

4 A Sorting

3.2.1 Data types

1 Changes an integer to a string. In this case, it evaluates to the string '16'.

2 Converts a real number to a string. In this case, it evaluates to the string '16.3'.

3 −9, 3, 5, 8, 98, 5,103

4 Processing speed: The time it takes a computer to calculate using 'real' numbers is a lot longer than for whole numbers held as integer data types.

Storage: Real data types take up more memory than integer data types; therefore if decimal points are not required it is better to use integers.

5 A real data type contains numeric data in a decimal form. It is used in situations where more accurate information is required than an integer can provide as an integer is a whole number.

6 Converts a string to a real data type. In this case it evaluates to the real 16.3

7 Storage: Real data types take up more memory than integer data types; therefore if decimal points are not required it is better to use integers.

The number has no decimals.

8 Changes a string to an integer. In this case, it evaluates to the integer 16.

3.2.2 Programming concepts

```
1 n ← 1
WHILE n ≤ 50
    OUTPUT n
    n ← n + 1
ENDWHILE
2 FOR n = 1 to 60
    OUTPUT n
ENDFOR
```

3 It is an independent set of statements, which can be called in another program. Each program segment is called a module.

```
4 OUTPUT "Please enter two numbers"
USERINPUT ← start
USERINPUT ← finish
FOR n = start to finish
    print n
ENDFOR
5 OUTPUT "Please enter the start
number"
USERINPUT ← start
OUTPUT "Please enter the end number"
USERINPUT ← finish
IF start > finish
```

```
    print "Your start number is larger
    than your end number"
ELSE
    FOR n = start to finish
        print n
    ENDFOR
ENDIF
6 a ← 1
REPEAT
OUTPUT a
a ← a + 1
UNTIL a = 6
# will output 1, 2, 3, 4, 5, 6
7 a ← 1
WHILE a < 4
    OUTPUT a
    a ← a + 1
ENDWHILE
# will output 1, 2, 3
8 FOR a ← 1 TO 3
    OUTPUT a
ENDFOR
# will output 1, 2, 3
```

3.2.3 Arithmetic operations in a programming language

1 B Logical operation

Operator	Description
+	PLUS
-	SUBTRACTION
*	MULTIPLICATION
/	DIVISION

```
3 9 DIV 5                    # evaluates to 1
4 9 MOD 5                    # evaluates to 4
```

3.2.4 Relational operations in a programming language

```
1 USERINPUT ← length
USERINPUT ← width
area ← length * width
perimeter ← 2*(length+width)
OUTPUT area
OUTPUT perimeter
2 OUTPUT "Please enter a number"
USERINPUT ← number
```

```
IF (number MOD 2) = 0 THEN
    OUTPUT "even"
ELSE
    OUTPUT "odd"
ENDIF
```

3

Operator	Description
>	Greater than
<	Less than
=	Equal to
≥	Greater than or equal to
≤	Less than or equal to
≠	Not equal to

```
4 OUTPUT "Please enter the size of your
  square"
  USERINPUT ← side
  IF side is negative
      OUTPUT "Length entered must be
      positive"
  ELSE
      print side*side
  ENDIF
5 OUTPUT "Please enter three numbers
  one at a time"
  USERINPUT ← a
  USERINPUT ← b
  USERINPUT ← c
  IF (a=b) and (a=c)
      OUTPUT "all 3 equal"
  ELSE
      OUTPUT "not all equal"
  ENDIF
6 OUTPUT "Please enter three numbers
  one at a time"
  USERINPUT ← a
  USERINPUT ← b
  USERINPUT ← c
  IF a>b
      bigab←a
  ELSE
      bigab←b
  ENDIF
  IF c>bigab
      OUTPUT c
  ELSE
      OUTPUT bigab
  ENDIF
```

3.2.5 Boolean operations in a programming language

```
1 If: "door is open" AND "cold outside"
  then "wear coat"
  or
  If: door=1 AND cold=1 then coat
2 a ← 2
  REPEAT
      OUTPUT a
      a ← a + 2
  UNTIL a = 102
```

3 The Boolean data type represents the values of true/false or yes/no. The primitive data type of a Boolean is logical. Boolean logic is a type of mathematical comparison. It is used to evaluate true or false. The lights could be on = 1 or off = 0.

3.2.6 Data structures

```
1 primes ← [2, 3, 5, 7, 11, 13]
```
2 A relatively permanent collections of data
```
3 primes[5] ← 17
  # array is now [2, 3, 5, 7, 11, 17]
```
4 Initialising an array means storing data in an array.

5 A one-dimensional array is a list of variables. To create an array, you first must define an array variable of the desired type. A one-dimensional array in Python and PHP is a data structure that allows a list of items to be stored with the capability of accessing each item by pointing to its location within the array, for example:

```
      carMakers ← ["Ford", "Land Rover",
      "Vauxhall", "Nissan", "Toyota"]
```

6 Two-dimensional arrays are a little more complex than one-dimensional arrays, but really they are nothing more than an array of arrays, in other words an array in one row and another in the next row.

7 It is common practice within programming for the first element within an array to be given an index of zero rather than 1, because 0 is considered by most mathematicians to be a real number between –1 and 1 and so in languages where arrays are positively indexed, zero is the first number (–1 is not possible, the first possible value then is 0).

8 This way the computer can keep track only of the address of the first element and the addresses of other elements can be calculated

```
9 tables ← [1, 2, 3],
            [2, 4, 6],
            [3, 6, 9],
            [4, 8, 12]]
```

10 9

3.2.7 Input/output and file handling

1 Sequential text files are stored like a one-dimensional array but they are read from start to finish and so cannot be read and written to simultaneously. They are readable across systems because they have a universal standard format that is used in all text editors.

Numerical data is always stored as a string, for example 5.32 would be stored as '5.32'.

2 Accessing data sequentially is much faster than accessing it randomly because of the way in which the disk hardware works. Because reading randomly involves a higher number of seek operations than a sequential reading, random reads deliver a lower rate of throughput. The same is true for random writing.

3.2.8 String-handling operations in a programming language

1 A string or text data type is capable of holding any alphanumeric character whether it is text, numbers or symbols. It is also capable of storing non-printable characters such as carriage returns as well as punctuation characters and spaces. The data contained within a string data type can either be pure text or consist of a combination of letters, numbers and symbols.

2 Evaluates to 'uter sc'

3 Evaluates to 'programmingiscool'

4 Converts a string to a real number. In this case evaluates to the real number '1.3'

3.2.9 Random number generation in a programming language

1 It will randomly generate 2, 3, 4, 5, 6, 7 or 8.

2 By definition a random number is something that cannot be predetermined or predicted in advance. You can program a machine to generate what can be called 'random' numbers, but the machine is always at the mercy of the programming used to generate the numbers which are always sequential. You can't generate anything you could really call a random sequence of numbers as the machine is following the same algorithm to generate them. They are therefore called 'pseudo-random' numbers.

3 Otherwise the program would do the same thing every time and often we need the computer to take a range of deferent pathways, particularly in gaming. They are useful not just for gaming

and simulation, but also in business. They can be used to produce unique Identifiers.

3.2.10 Subroutines (procedures and functions)

1 A function is a small segment of a program (sub-program) designed to perform a specific task and return a result to the main or calling program.

2 The term "word length" refers to the number of bits processed by a computer's CPU in one go. Whilst it used to be 8 bits, with modern CPUs it is now typically 32 bits or 64 bits.

4 Information or values that are passed to the function through special identifiers are called arguments.

5 The arguments (values) which are passed to the function when a function call is made are called actual parameters.

6 The arguments which are used in the argument list of the function header to receive the values from the calling program are called formal parameters or dummy parameters.

7 A function is invoked (or called) through an output statement or an assignment statement by using the function name followed by the list of arguments. For example:

```
p = prod(x, y);
```

8 Variables declared inside a block or function are said to belong only to that block and these are called local variables. Values of these variables are valid only in that block.

9 Variables declared before the main function block are called global variables. Values of these variables are available in every block of that program. Global variables are the data that are declared before the main program and that are available to the main program as well as the functions that are called from the main program.

3.2.11 Structured programming

1 • Sequence
  • Selection
  • Iteration

2 It is an independent set of statements, which can be called in another program. Each program segment is called a module.

3 It is a method of using the concept of sequence, selection, iteration and modularity.

4 • Modifications are limited to module.
  • Increases programmer's productivity.

5 • Structured programs are easy to write as the programming logic is well organised.
  • Structured programs are easy to test and debug.

6 • To produce error-free programs.
  • To incorporate basic structured constructs.
  • To eliminate use of GOTO statements.
  • To obtain a disciplined approach towards programming.
  • To improve the flexibility of a program.

7 A structure is a group of data of different data types.

8 An array of structures contains data elements of every structure variable stored in an array.

3.2.12 Robust and secure programming

1 • Syntax errors
  • Runtime errors
  • Logic errors

2 The correct name is syntax error and it relates to the grammar rules of the programming language used. These errors are usually due to using the wrong case, placing punctuation in positions where it should not exist or failing to insert punctuation where it should be placed within the code.

3 Called 'runtime errors' these occur whenever the program instructs the computer to carry out an operation that it is either not designed to do or slow to do. They cause a crash or slow running of the code.

4 Logic errors are the most difficult kind of errors to detect and rectify. This is usually down to the fact that there is no obvious indication of the error within the software. The program will run successfully; however, it will not behave in the manner it was designed to. In other words, it will simply produce incorrect results.

5 Dry-run testing is usually carried out on the algorithm which is written in pseudo-code or as part of a flowchart. This form of testing is usually done prior to the program code being written.

6 A trace table is a technique used to test algorithms to see if any logic errors are occurring whilst the algorithm is being processed. Within the table, each column contains a variable and each row displays each numerical input into the algorithm and the resultant values of the variables.

7 B Debugging

3.2.13 Classification of programming languages

1 B Object code is saved for future use
2 C assembler

3 C compiler
4 B A compiler converts the whole of a high-level program code into machine code in one step
5 A machine language

3.3.2 Converting between number bases

1 A binary
2 C decimal
3 B octal
4 D hexadecimal
5 B 1

3.3.3 Units of information

1 C 4 bits
2 B 8 bits
3 D 1 KB = 1,000 bytes
4 A binary digits
5 C eight bits
6 A 1,000 bytes
7 C 1,000 megabytes
8 B 1 petabyte

3.3.4 Binary arithmetic

1

Addition	Answer
101 + 11 =	00001000
111 + 111 =	00001110
1010 + 1010 =	00010100
11101 + 1010 =	00100111
11111 + 11111 =	00111110

3.3.5 Character encoding

1 A American Standard Code for Information Interchange
2 C 7
3 Converts the character to a character code. In this case, it evaluates to 97 using ASCII/Unicode.
4 Converts the character code to a character. In this case, it evaluates to 'a' using ASCII/Unicode.
5 A ASCII
6 Extended ASCII uses all 8 bits whereas ASCII just uses 7. This means it can store more characters.

7 Unlike ASCII's 128 characters and 7 bits, Unicode can store each character with 32 bits so contains over 110,000 characters and has space for 1,114,111 different values that can be used for characters. Because of this it can store foreign language characters. The first 128 character are the same as ASCII.

3.3.6 Representing images

1 Analogue data is continuous, analogous to the actual information it represents. For example, a mercury thermometer is an analogue device. The mercury rises in direct proportion to the temperature. Computers cannot work with analogue information.

Digital data breaks the information up into separate parts. This is done by breaking the analogue information into pieces and representing those pieces using binary digits.

2 **D** All of the above

3 **Step 1:** (Length × Width) × bit depth = (800 × 900) × 24 bits = 17,280,000 bits

Step 2: Convert into appropriate units

$$\frac{17,280,000}{8} = 2,160,000 \text{ bytes}$$

$$\frac{2,160,000 \text{ bytes}}{1,000} = 2,160 \text{ kB}$$

$$\frac{2,160 \text{ kB}}{1,000} = 2.1 \text{ MB}$$

4 800 × 600 is 480,000 pixels. Each pixel takes 3 bytes (one byte each for red/green/blue), so 480,000 × 3 = 1,440,000 bytes overall, which is approximately 1.4 MB, therefore this is the space required for the image in RAM. On disk a jpg file takes up much less space than that; this is due to 'compression' which is an effective space-saving technique for image and audio data.

3.3.7 Representing sound

1 60 minutes per hour, 20 × 60 = 1,200 minutes

So that's about 1,200 MB, which is 1.2 GB

2 In analogue recordings, the machine is constantly recording any sound or noise that is coming through the microphones. In digital recording, you don't have a constant recording, you have a series of samples or snapshots which are a measure of amplitude at a given point in time and are taken from the sound being recorded.

3.3.8 Data compression

1 If we will look at a sentence such as 'run-length encoding makes files smaller; smaller files use run-length encoding' we would notice that each character and space in this sentence made up one unit of memory. So we would have a file size of 78 bytes. There are regular patterns in our sentence as most of the words appear twice with the exception of 'makes' and 'use' which appear just once. If we create a dictionary, we can catalogue the words so we do not need to repeat them, just call up the catalogue location.

2 Run-length encoding is a data compression algorithm used in most bitmap file formats. This system is used in TIFF, BMP and PCX file formats. RLE works by reducing the size of a repeating string. A repeating string is called a run and is typically encoded into two bytes. The first byte represents the number of characters in the run and is called the run count. The second byte is the value of the character in the run and is called the run value.

RLE is suitable for compressing any type of data. The problem is that the content of the data affects the compression ratio as it depends on the number of repeats in the string; the more repeats the more effective the compression.

3 Data compression is a set of steps for packing data into a smaller 'electronic space' (data bits). Compression results in much smaller storage space requirements and is often much faster for communications, as compressed data works more effectively on our mobile phones and portable devices. But to be effective we still need to allow for the original data to be accessed and used. This is often achieved by eliminating the repetition of identical sets of data bits. We call this removing the "redundancy".

4 Sort the symbols into descending order by frequency.

Merge the two least frequent symbols, with the lower symbol as the root and combined frequency as frequency.

Repeat until the tree is complete.

3.4.1 Hardware and software 1

1 It carries a word to or from memory.

2 It carries a memory address. The width of an address bus equals the number of bits in the MAR.

3 **D** All of the above

3.4.1 Hardware and software 2

1 It is used to store intermediate data and instructions.

2 It keeps track of the memory address of the instruction that is to be executed next.

3 **C** read-only memory chip

4 **D** Any of the above

5 **D** Microprocessor

6 **B** CD-ROM

7 **C** control unit, arithmetic-logic unit and primary storage

8 **B** Output unit

9 **A** Arithmetic Logic Unit

3.4.2 Boolean logic

1

The tyre is flat.	The wheel has been removed.	Take the wheel to the garage.
1	1	1
1	0	0
0	1	0
0	0	0

2

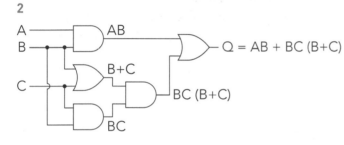

3

AND gate

A	B	Q
0	0	0
0	1	0
1	0	0
1	1	1

INPUT   OUTPUT

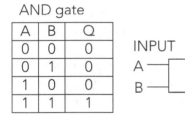

OR gate

A	B	Q
0	0	0
0	1	1
1	0	1
1	1	1

INPUT   OUTPUT

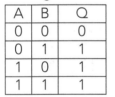

3.4.3 Software classification 1

1 **D** Entertainment software

2 **B** application software

3 **A** system software

4 **C** compiler

5 **C** Diagnostic software

6 **D** Assembly languages

7 **A** High-level language

3.4.3 Software classification 2

1 The operating system is actually not one, but a collection of programs that control the system. The operating system is responsible for the management and control of all the computer's resources. This includes memory, processors, hard drives, monitoring I/O devices, etc. It not only handles the system resources, it also handles the application software that users run, security and file management. It also provides a link between the hardware and software.

2 The operating system memory management functions include controlling the location of memory, dealing with the transfer of programs in and out of memory when the process no longer needs it or when the process has been ended. It also carries out a process called scheduling where it manages the CPU, organising the use of memory between programs and organises processing time between programs and users. The OS also keeps track of processors and the status of any process running.

3 It is one of the main functions of the operating system – managing the input to the CPU and the output from the CPU.

3.4.4 Systems architecture 1

1 **D** arithmetic logic and control unit

2 Cache memory is a small and fast memory between CPU and main memory. It is extremely fast compared to normal memory. Transferring data between main memory and CPU causes delay because RAM is slower than CPU. Cache memory stores copies of data from most frequently used main memory locations. When processor needs to read from or write to a location in main memory, it first checks whether a copy of data is in the cache. If so the processor immediately reads or writes to cache. Computers use multi-levels of cache such as Level 1 (smallest) and Level 2 cache. CPU resident cache is known as L1 or primary cache (16 to 32 kB) to 512 kB. Cache is also added to the motherboard, also known as L2 cache (512 kB to 1,024 kB). Higher end systems can have as much as 2 MB of L2 cache on the motherboard.

3 **A** Input unit

4 **A** Electrically Erasable Programmable Read Only Memory

5 **A** ALU

6 **A** Seek time + latency time

7 CPU speed/clock speed: speed of CPU also known as clock speed. The clock speed is the number of instructions executed by the CPU in one second. It is measured in megahertz (million instructions per second). The average speed of a new CPU is about 1,000 MHz to 4,000 MHz (1 to 4 gigahertz).

Instruction set: The number of instructions decides the efficiency of a CPU. The greater number of instructions, the less efficient is the CPU and fewer instructions, the more efficient is the CPU.

Word size/Register size: The size of registers determines the amount of data the computer can work with at a time. The smaller the size of the register, the slower will be the computer. It is also known as Word size. It varies from 16 bits to 128 bits.

Data bus capacity: The width of the data bus determines the largest number of bits that can be transported at one time.

Cache memory size: Cache memory is a high-speed memory. The larger the cache, the faster a processor runs. Most modern processors can execute multiple instructions per clock cycle which speeds up a program. Some CPUs have storage for instructions and data built inside the processor chip. This is called the internal cache or L1 cache memory.

Memory size: The amount of primary storage (RAM) determines the size of program that can be kept in primary storage, which is faster than secondary storage. Thereby the speed of the computer increases. The size of RAM varies.

8 Program counter: This register stores the address of the next instruction to be executed.

Memory address register (MAR): This register specifies the address in memory where information can be found. This register is also used to point to a memory location where information can be stored.

Memory buffer register: This register acts as an interface between CPU and memory. A Read Memory command causes an instruction to be fetched and placed in the MB register.

9 C ALU

10 D all of these

3.4.4 Systems architecture 2

1 D All of the above
2 D Compact Disk Read Only Memory
3 A Input unit
4 C Loads a program from the disk into the memory
5 D all of these

3.5.1 Fundamentals of computer networks 1

1 It is the interconnection of autonomous computers and terminals together using communication systems to facilitate exchange of information.

2 It is the main component of the network. It is a very fast computer with a large amount of RAM and storage space. A file server stores all the files and application software and operating system.

3 It is also referred to as a node, work stations (also referred to as clients) are the computers connected to the file server.

4 B Wide Area Network

5 A router translates information from one network to another. Routers select the best path to route a message based on the destination address and origin.

6 It is a device that provides a central connection point to cables from a server's workstations and peripherals.

7 • Serial transmission method
   • Parallel transmission method

8 It is a physical layout of the cables, arrangement of resources and communication facilities.

9 Advantages:
   • Network allows users to share software stored in a main system.
   • Site (network) software licenses are less expensive than buying several standalone licenses.
   • Files can easily be shared between users over a network.
   • Network users can communicate via email, instant messenger, and VoiP.
   • Security over networks is of a high standard, i.e. users cannot see other users' files, unlike on stand-alone machines.
   • Within networks, it is much more straightforward to backup data as it is all stored on the file server.
   • Networks allow data to be transmitted to remote areas that are connected within local areas.
   • Networking computers allows users to share common peripheral resources such as printers, fax machines, modems etc. therefore saving money.
   • The cost of computing is reduced per user as compared with the development and maintenance of a group of un-networked standalone computers.

   Disadvantages:
   • The cabling to construct a network as well as the file servers can be costly.
   • The management of a large network is complicated, which requires training and a specialist network manager usually needs to be employed.
   • In the event of a file server breaking down the files contained on the server become inaccessible, although email might still work if it is stored on a separate email server. The computers can still be used but are isolated.

- If a virus gets into the system it can easily spread to other computers in the network.
- With networks, there is a risk of hacking, particularly with wide area networks. Stringent security measures are required to prevent such abuse, such as a firewall.

3.5.1 Fundamentals of computer networks 2

1 IMAP is a mail retrieval protocol with improvements over POP. The main advantage is you can keep emails on the mail server instead of always downloading them.
2 POP is used for downloading emails to a local PC; it operates at the application layer.
3 Simple Mail Transfer Protocol is used for sending email; it operates at the application layer.
4 This protocol operates at the network layer of the OSI model and is involved in network routing and addressing.

3.6.1 Cyber security threats 1

1 Phishing is trying to trick someone into revealing confidential information, such as passwords and account numbers, by imitating a company or website the user would normally be familiar with.
2 Shoulder surfing is to have someone stealing confidential information simply by looking over your shoulder while you're accessing it.
3 Pharming is when a user is misdirected to an attack website, without their knowledge, by code that has been previously installed on their computer that modifies their destination URL to one chosen by the attacker.
4 Spam is unsolicited email. It is usually more of an annoyance than a security threat. Spam wastes time, employee resources and bandwidth.
5 This is a human or software-based attack in which the goal is to pretend to be someone else for the purpose of concealing their identity. Spoofing can occur by using IP addresses, a network adapter's hardware media access control (MAC) address and email.
6 This is a human-based attack in which an attacker pretends to be someone he is not.

3.6.1 Cyber security threats 1

1 Propagation and destruction. The propagation function defines how the virus will spread from system to system. The destructive power is caused by implementing whatever malicious activity the virus writer had in mind.

2 Viruses are a collection of coded instructions which are self-replicating. When a virus attaches itself to another file it infects it. The virus is normally inactive until an infected program is run.
Viruses are broadly classified into three categories:
- Boot infectors create bad sectors. They remain in the memory until the system is shutdown.
- System infectors infect the hard disk or bootable floppies which may contain system files.
- Executable program infectors are dangerous and devastating. They spread to almost any executable program attaching themselves to programming files.
3 It is a malware software program that appears benevolent but carries a malicious, behind-the-scenes payload that has the potential to wreak havoc on a system or network.
4 Worms replicate themselves without requiring any human intervention, viruses do not.
5 Spyware monitors your actions and transmits important details to a remote system that spies on your activity.
6 Adware uses a variety of techniques to display advertisements on infected computers' active content.
7 A security breach that is caused or facilitated by someone who is a part of the very organisation that controls or builds the asset that should be protected.

3.6.2 Methods to detect and prevent cyber security threats

1 Threats
- Privacy
- Integrity
- Environmental damage
- Human threats
- Software threats
- Unauthorised access
- Computer viruses

Security
- Physical protection of machine and media
- Using passwords and users
- Using licensed software
- Use of cryptography

2 By not applying a patch you might be leaving the door open for malware to come in. Malware exploits flaws in a system in order to do its work and updates and patches are designed to close these doors as they are found. Applying patches often also addresses technical issues with the software and improves the software's performance.

3   Both the TLS and SSL protocols use an 'asymmetric' Public Key Infrastructure (PKI) system.

When the school's browser requests an HTTPS connection, the website will first send its SSL certificate to the browser. This certificate contains the public key needed to begin a secure data session. Based on this initial exchange, the browser and the website then initiate an 'SSL handshake'.

3.7 Ethical, legal and environmental impacts of digital technology on wider society, including issues of privacy

1   In the last ten years there has been some major changes in the way we shop due to new online shopping environments being launched, coupled with the expanding availability of super-fast broadband to people's homes. This now means that people can sit at home and buy the things that they want. The ease in which people can now shop online has caused a big shift in the products that shoppers most desire. Recent statistics have shown that technology such as tablet computers and home communication packages (TV/broadband/phone) are the most wanted items by people living in the UK.

2   Some of the world's best security researchers had been threatened with legal action for their efforts to expose vulnerabilities in internet infrastructure. The law tries to prevent hacking, or breaking into private networks and systems. But internet security experts use hacking projects to uncover security flaws with the intention of fixing them. Many people believe that cyber-crime laws should take into account the intent behind hacking, and not just the act itself.

We willingly give up our personal data on a daily basis, to services such as Facebook and Google. In these cases, our data isn't being stolen from us. As with all moral issues about internet privacy, there are two sides to the story – that of the person giving up their private data, and that of the person storing it.

A key feature of the internet that affects our privacy is the net's inability to forget anything once posted there. Web pages about individuals often stay online and searchable indefinitely, potentially affecting the subject's reputation.

Another way that every internet user's privacy is infringed is by government surveillance. The governments of most nations tap internet traffic as part of national security programmes.